D1523459

The Talmud
of the
Land of Israel

Chicago Studies in the History of Judaism
Edited by Jacob Neusner,
William Scott Green,
and Calvin Goldscheider

The University of Chicago Press
Chicago and London

The Talmud of the Land of Israel

A Preliminary Translation and Explanation

Volume 16   Rosh Hashanah

Translated by
Edward A. Goldman

EDWARD GOLDMAN is professor of Rabbinic literature at the
Hebrew Union College—Jewish Institute of Religion, Cincinnati.

The University of Chicago Press, Chicago 60637
The University of Chicago Press, Ltd., London

© 1988 by The University of Chicago
All rights reserved. Published 1988
Printed in the United States of America

97 96 95 94 93 92 91 90 89 88   54321

Library of Congress Cataloging-in-Publication Data

Talmud Yerushalmi. Rosh ha-shanah.
  Rosh hashanah.

  (The Talmud of the land of Israel; v. 16)
(Chicago studies in the history of Judaism)
  Includes bibliographical references and indexes.
  1. Talmud Yerushalmi. Rosh ha-shanah—Criticism,
Textual. I. Goldman, Edward A., 1941–   . II. Title.
III. Series: Talmud Yerushalmi. English. 1982; v. 16.
IV. Series: Chicago studies in the history of Judaism.
BM498.5.E5 1982 vol. 16   296.1'2407 s   87-18213
ISBN 0-226-57675-2   [BM506.R5] [296.1'24]

For
Roanete
Ariel and Dalia

Contents

Foreword   ix

Acknowledgments   xiii

Introduction to Rosh Hashanah   1

1   Mishnah Rosh Hashanah, Chapter One   11

2   Mishnah Rosh Hashanah, Chapter Two   55

3   Mishnah Rosh Hashanah, Chapter Three   76

4   Mishnah Rosh Hashanah, Chapter Four   96

Index of Biblical and Talmudic References   119

General Index   121

Foreword

The opportunity to be a participant in this Palestinian Talmud series has made it possible for me to complete a cherished project begun many years ago. From 1975 to 1978, I published in the *Hebrew Union College Annual* (vols. 46–49) seriatim the four chapters of "A Critical Edition of Palestinian Talmud Tractate Rosh Hashanah." That work was undertaken to determine a coherent and accurate text based upon manuscripts and genizah fragments. Parallel texts from elsewhere in the rabbinic literature and even citations from some early commentators were also included to aid in recovering the original wording and/or sense of the passages. Because in many instances the printed texts are problematic, my first priority was "to provide a text which would be an improvement upon the printed Venice edition, the Cracow, the Krotoschin, or the other printed texts which derive from the Venice edition."[1] My second priority has now also been reached—an annotated translation based upon that critical text.

My goal, whether in the Hebrew-Aramaic critical text or in the translation, has been to help the student of rabbinic literature to achieve a better understanding and greater appreciation of one "Yerushalmi" tractate. A translation of this kind is not the appropriate place to draw overarching conclusions about the Palestinian Talmud, or about life in the land of Israel from the third to the fifth centuries C.E. I hope that the material included here, both the text in translation and the notes, can help serve as a source for such studies. I saw my role as providing a mine to be worked.

1. *HUCA* 46 (1975), p. 222.

The Method of This Study

As mentioned above, the *HUCA* critical text forms the basis for this translation. For that project, I used the Leiden manuscript[2] which belongs to the Bibliothecae Academiae Lugduno-Batavae as my main text. The Leiden MS is particularly valuable because it served as the basis for the *editio princeps*, the printed Venice edition.[3] In addition, the editors of the Venice edition referred to three other manuscripts they had before them.[4] The reason I used the Leiden MS rather than the Venice edition is that one can see in the manuscript itself marginal notes and editorial markings and changes which were then incorporated into the printed text. One can reconstruct many of the editorial decisions leading to the Venice edition by seeing what constituted the pristine primary text, what represented glosses by another hand that the editors chose to rely upon, and what must have represented changes based upon the editors' own discretion or reliance upon traditions in their other three manuscripts. One is then in a better position to separate out "correct original readings changed by an editor, or editorial additions which were not entered into the text in the correct place. Sometimes we find that the editor did not completely fill in an incomplete reading. *Memrot* have been left out of the Venice edition; on occasion the printer erred in reading the manuscript or even the editorial notes and glosses."[5] Accuracy was therefore best served by working from the original rather than from a less reliable copy.

Anyone interested in knowing my methodology for the critical text will find it spelled out in *HUCA* 46, pp. 219–27. That text is numbered by page and line of the Leiden MS to facilitate easy reference. It is also paragraphed for the purpose of separating thought units and providing an easy vehicle for referring to a specific location in the text or for quoting.

This translation uses the paragraphing system of the critical text so that ready reference to the Hebrew-Aramaic there can be

2. Leiden MS Cod. Scal. 3
3. *Talmud Yerushalmi . . . Venezia*, Daniel Bomberg, 1523–24. Reprinted without place or date. Second offset printing, Berlin, 1925.
4. An editorial paragraph appended at the very end of the Venice edition indicates this. At the end of the Gemara for tractate Shabbat, another editorial comment indicates that four old manuscript copies were utilized for this work. Although the Leiden MS was clearly the main text, the editors may have utilized three other manuscripts no longer extant for corrections.
5. Goldman, *HUCA* 46, p. 221.

made. The paragraphs serve to identify thought units, and also
to simplify precise citation of units. I deeply appreciate the will-
ingness of the editor, Jacob Neusner, to permit a format which
differs from his own reference system. He understood my need
to have units which conform to my reference text, and he gra-
ciously allowed me this flexibility. For those who are studying
the translation with a printed text, the standard units of chapter
and halakhah are included, as well as page and column in the
Krotoschin edition.

My methodological goal in translating was to render the
Hebrew-Aramaic into as literal an English as possible while
maintaining linguistic fluency. Additions in square brackets were
limited to those instances where they were necessary to achieve
smooth flow and readability of the text, or comprehension. Ex-
planatory material and comments are limited to the footnotes at
the bottom of the page, again to enhance and to simplify the
usability of the text proper. Those who wish to read the text
along with the detailed notes will do so; those who merely want
to read a textual translation can do so without encumbrance.
The purpose of this system is to facilitate the readers' use of it
on the level they wish. Again, thanks are in order to Jacob
Neusner for allowing this variation in format.

My translation represents an eclectic text. I have consistently
attempted to utilize *what I considered* the best readings for each
unit. Usually I translate directly from the Leiden MS, but only
after checking all the other available manuscripts, genizah fragments, parallel texts, etc. Occasionally I find that a parallel text,
perhaps even in the same manuscript, provides a reading that
makes better sense. I adopted the guiding principle that the text
was intended to make sense and to flow logically. Therefore
when choices are to be made, I select those options that *from my
perspective* render maximum coherence. I utilize suggestions by
P'ne Moshe,[6] Korban Ha'edah,[7] Saul Lieberman, and Zev Wolf
Rabinovitz[8] in precisely the same way. When I do depart from
Rosh Hashanah of the Leiden MS, I indicate in the footnotes
what I have done in order to allow the reader to make an independent judgment.

6. Moses Margolies (d. 1780). Amsterdam: 1754; Leghorn: 1770. Reprinted
in the Palestinian Talmud.
7. David Frankel (d. 1762). Mo'ed, Dessau: 1743; Nashim, Berlin: 1757;
Nezikin, Berlin: 1760. Reprinted in the Palestinian Talmud.
8. Z. W. Rabinovitz, *Sha'are Torath Eretz Israel*, Jerusalem, 1940.

My comments and notes on the Mishnah are not extensive. Many excellent aids for Mishnah study already exist, and therefore someone who wants to study the Mishnah for its own sake would be well advised to use one or more of the extant works. My interest here is in how the Palestinian Talmud understands and utilizes the Mishnah, and to this end my comments are limited.

Transliteration

In order to render Hebrew words into the most easily recognizable romanizations, I have generally utilized the "More Exact Romanization Style" outlined in table 2, p. 11, of *American National Standard: Romanization of Hebrew* (New York, 1975). On occasion, I have used table 1, p. 9, "General-Purpose Romanization Style." For commonly used words such as the names of holidays, or names of Mishnah or Talmud tractates, I utilize the general word-lists in *How Do You Spell Chanukah? A General-Purpose Romanization of Hebrew for Speakers of English* by Werner Weinberg (Cincinnati: Hebrew Union College Press, 1976).

Proper Names

Transcribing names in the Palestinian Talmud poses special problems. Many names appear with several variations, for example, Abba and Ba, Abun and Bun, Yosé, Yosa and Yasa, Yehuda, Yoda, and Yodan. One can either romanize each variation exactly as it appears, or settle upon one English rendering for each name. I have chosen the latter course.

Acknowledgments

Many friends and colleagues have contributed greatly to this work in its many phases. Ben Zion Wacholder read the entire Hebrew-Aramaic critical text, and guided me in that stage of the project. He also read and commented upon Chapter 1 of the translation, and was readily available for questions and consultations on the rest. Eugene Mihaly read Chapter 1 of the critical text and the translation, and he made many important suggestions. He also has been a ready source of advice on difficult passages in the other three chapters. To these men, my teachers and HUC colleagues, I am deeply indebted.

Moshe Assis, of the Department of Talmud at Tel Aviv University and one of the foremost Yerushalmi scholars in the world, has been most generous with his time and advice. He read and commented upon Chapters 2, 3, and 4 of the critical text. He also served as one of the critical readers for this volume. I am most grateful for his many invaluable corrections and comments.

My HUC colleague Stephen Kaufman served as the second critical reader of this volume. He brought to bear upon the translation his enormous knowledge of Hebrew and Aramaic. His corrections and comments were incisive and significant. I greatly appreciate his help.

Needless to say, translation of necessity implies interpretation, and this is particularly true of the Palestinian Talmud. The text is occasionally enigmatic, sometimes problematic, and highly apocopated. Often the commentators and students of these texts do not agree as to their meaning. The ultimate responsibility, then, for rendering the meaning is my own. Whatever faults or insufficiencies exist in this work are mine.

A word of thanks is due my typists. Edith Goffin typed Chapters 1 and 2. Janet Schroeder typed Chapters 3 and 4, and made the many editorial revisions that were necessary throughout the text. I am grateful to them for their meticulous hard work and their patience.

And finally, special thanks are due to Jacob Neusner, the person who envisioned this series and is carrying it through to completion. All of us who are participants in the project and/or students of the Palestinian Talmud are indebted to him for his contribution to Yerushalmi scholarship.

Introduction to Rosh Hashanah

Mishnah Rosh Hashanah deals essentially with two issues: (1) the most significant of the four New Years, and the specifics for sanctifying the New Moon which are necessary because *The Rosh Hashanah* is a New Moon; (2) the sounding of the shofar on *The Rosh Hashanah,* and the specifics regarding the shofar to be used and the liturgical details related to the sounding. Each of these issues flows directly from Scriptures, and so an examination of the relevant verses is necessary.

Leviticus 23:1–2 introduces the year's calendar of sacred occasions: "The Lord spoke to Moses, saying: Speak to the Israelite people and say to them: These are My fixed times, the fixed times of the Lord, which you shall proclaim as sacred occasions." The Gemara in Chapter 3, Halakhah 1, comments upon the tension between (1) "the fixed times of the Lord" (2) "which you shall proclaim."

Leviticus 23:23–25 reads as follows:

> The Lord spoke to Moses, saying: Speak to the Israelite people thus: In the seventh month, on the first day of the month, you shall observe complete rest, a sacred occasion commemorated with loud blasts. You shall not work at your occupations; you shall bring an offering by fire to the Lord.

Here, in the prescription for *The Rosh Hashanah,* we see that it is a New Moon "commemorated with loud blasts." Numbers 10:10 supports the connection between New Moons and loud blasts. "And on your joyous occasions, your fixed festivals and New Moon days, you shall sound the trumpets over your burnt offerings and your sacrifices of well-being. They shall be a reminder to you before the Lord your God: I, the Lord, am your God.”

Numbers 29:1 also indicates that *The Rosh Hashanah* is a New Moon, and "a day when the horn is sounded." There the sacrifices are detailed.

> In the seventh month, on the first day of the month, you shall observe a sacred occasion: You shall not work at your occupations. You shall observe it as a day when the horn is sounded. You shall present a burnt offering of pleasing odor to the Lord: one bull of the herd, one ram, and seven yearling lambs, without blemish. The meal offering with them—choice flour with oil mixed in— shall be: three-tenths of a measure for a bull, two-tenths for a ram, and one-tenth for each of the seven lambs. And there shall be one goat for a sin offering, to make expiation in your behalf— in addition to the burnt offering of the New Moon with its meal offering and the regular burnt offering with its meal offering, each with its libation as prescribed, offerings by fire of pleasing odor to the Lord.

Another key scriptural passage which links *The Rosh Hashanah* to the sounding of the shofar is Psalms 81:2–5. Chapter 1, Halakhah 3, paragraph 7 quotes Rav's *Shofar Prayers*: "today is the day of the beginning of your works, a memorial to the first day [of creation]. 'For it is a statute for Israel, an ordinance of the God of Jacob'" (Psalms 81:5). The previous verse, Psalms 81:4, reads: "Blow the horn at the New Moon, at the full moon for our feast-day." Hence the reference is to *The Rosh Hashanah*. The interpretation of Psalms 81:5 is also central to Halakhah 3, paragraph 28.

The above verses provide the central themes of the tractate, but the Mishnah and Gemara expand widely upon these themes. Here is a brief outline of the tractate.

There Are Four New Years (1:1–1:3)

1:1–2   The Mishnah prologue lists four different dates from which one might begin the year, depending upon the purpose. The Gemara devotes the first eighteen paragraphs to proving that the year begins with Nisan. The scriptural verse which provides the basis for this discussion is Exodus 12:2: "This month shall mark for you the beginning of the months; it shall be the first of the months of the year for you." It is further shown that Nisan is the beginning of regnal years, and paragraphs 19 and 20 demonstrate the use of regnal years in notes. Paragraphs 21 through 25 attempt to reconcile King David's regnal years in Scriptures.

According to the Mishnah, the first of Nisan is also the New Year for the order of festivals; paragraphs 26 through 53 explore the implications. To the reign of kings and the order of festivals which the Mishnah counts from the first of Nisan, the Rabbis add the payment of rent and the offering of the shekel. Paragraph 54 deals with rent; 55 to 57, the shekel.

Paragraph 58 returns to the next phrase of the Mishnah, "On the first of Elul is the New Year for the Tithe of Cattle. . . ." The discussion of tithing continues through paragraph 71, the end of Halakhah 1.

Mishnah 2, following the numbering of the Leiden MS, continues with the New Year which is on the first of Tishri. Paragraphs 1 through 4 explore the basis for establishing the first of Tishri as the New Year for the reckoning of years; paragraph 5—Sabbaticals; paragraphs 6 through 8—Jubilees. Because the fruit of young trees was forbidden for common use during the first three years as being *orlah* (Leviticus 19:23), a point from which one might count the New Year for young trees was also necessary and the Mishnah designates the first of Tishri. This is explored in paragraphs 9 through 13. The first of Tishri is also the New Year for vegetables to be tithed—paragraph 14. The remainder of Halakhah 2 deals with the date of the New Year for fruit trees.

1:3   Mishnah 3 (again following the numbering of the Leiden MS) continues the prologue of the four New Years by itemizing another "four," in this case four judgment-times which occur during the year for different purposes: Passover for grain, the Festival of Weeks for fruit, *The Rosh Hashanah* for humans, and Tabernacles for water. The entire Halakhah deals with these four judgments.

The New Moon (1:4–3:1)

1:4   Mishnah 4 catalogues the six New Moons (seven when the Temple stood) on which messengers went forth to distant places after the Court had received testimony concerning the appearance of the new moon and had proclaimed the new month. Clearly these distant communities had to know whether the previous month had been 29 or 30 days so that they could observe holidays at the proper time. Halakhah 4 examines the need for messengers on Rosh Ḥodesh Sivan and Tishri. In paragraph 3, Rabbi Joshua ben Levi assures the safety of messengers who go to Nimrin in Syria. The residents of Nimrin, the last station for messengers, are concerned about getting the information lest they have to fast for two days of Yom Kippur (paragraph 4). The father of Rabbi Samuel ben Rav Isaac actually fasted two days and died (paragraph 5).

1:5   Mishnah 5 teaches that on two New Moons witnesses may violate the Sabbath prohibitions in order to travel to the Court for testimony. An early start in these months is critical for the messengers. While the Temple stood, however, witnesses could violate the Sabbath prohibitions in any month because of the need to determine the New Moon offering.

1:6   Mishnah 6 teaches that witnesses may violate the Sabbath prohibitions whether or not the New Moon was seen clearly. Rabbi Jose demurs, claiming that if it was seen clearly, there is no need to profane the Sabbath, presumably because it would have been seen clearly at the location of the Court as well.

1:7   Mishnah 7 and Halakhah 6 are an outgrowth of Mishnah 6. Rabbi Akiba detained forty pairs of witnesses in Lod so as to prevent unnecessary desecration of the Sabbath. Rabban Gamaliel rebuked him because widespread community participation in the moon-witnessing procedure was deemed so important.

1:8–9   Mishnah 8 also stresses the importance of participation in the moon-witnessing process. A father and a son who saw the New Moon should both go to testify, even though they cannot testify together to constitute the required two witnesses because of their relationship. Rabbi Simon argues that a father and a son, as well as all relatives, are eligible for testimony concerning the New Moon. Halakhah 7 supports Rabbi Simon's position with Exodus 12:1, where God shows the brothers Moses and Aaron the New Moon. Mishnah 9 and Halakhah 8 show that the priests agreed with Rabbi Simon's position, whereas the Court agreed with the anonymous position of the Mishnah.

1:10   Mishnah 10 lists those unqualified to be witnesses, which would include testifying concerning the New Moon. Halakhah 9 further defines those who are disqualified and tells what they must do to become eligible. In paragraph 8, four groups are added to those declared ineligible in the Mishnah.

1:11   Mishnah 11 and Halakhah 10 show the extent to which profanation of the Sabbath is permitted to further the goal of getting witnesses to go and testify. Mishnahs 4 through 11 all implicitly or explicitly stress the importance of getting witnesses, and hence the importance of the moon-witnessing process itself.

2:1   If the Court in Jerusalem is not going to recognize the witness, his local community sends a character witness with him to attest to his credibility. Paragraphs 1 and 2 of the Gemara examine the word order of the Mishnah. Paragraphs 3 through 9 address the question of whether one character witness from his hometown suffices. Paragraph 10 asks whether the character witnesses, like the moon witnesses themselves, can profane the Sabbath.

The second sentence of the Mishnah explains why character witnesses were necessary if the moon witnesses weren't known to the Court. Originally they would accept testimony about the New Moon from any man; after the *minim* ruined that system, the Court would accept testimony only from persons known (or else attested). Paragraphs 11 through 13 of the Gemara identify the *minim* and their intentions.

The third sentence of the Mishnah explains why messengers went forth when a practical and efficient signal-fire system was already in place. Paragraphs 14 through 17 elaborate upon the discontinuance of the beacon network. Paragraphs 18 through 20 tell when the beacons had been lit when the system was operative.

2:2   Mishnah 2 first tells how and of what the beacons were constructed, and then tells how they were waved. Paragraphs 1 and 2 of Halakhah 2 elaborate.

2:3   Mishnah 3 describes the network of signal stations. Paragraph 3 adds two more stations to those mentioned in the Mishnah, and describes the view of the diaspora from the top of Bet Baltin, the final station.

2:4–5   Mishnahs 4 and 5 give the physical location and circumstances of the witnesses in Jerusalem. They gathered and were examined in a large courtyard called Bet Ya'azek. Halakhah 3 examines the derivation of the name. Abundant meals were prepared for them as an added inducement for the trip. Rabban Gamaliel loosened the former restraints on their Sabbath travel after examination, so that they might walk two thousand cubits in any direction. Others for whom Gamaliel's leniency applied are also listed. Halakhah 4 elaborates.

2:6–7   Mishnahs 6 and 7 tell how the witnesses were examined. Mishnah 6 lists the questions directed to the first witness. Paragraphs 1 and 2 of Halakhah 5 interpret the first question. Paragraphs 3 through 8 represent a midrashic excursus on the harmony and order in God's upper reaches. Paragraphs 9 through 11 stress that witnesses must see the moon directly, not a reflection, not through the clouds. Paragraphs 12 and 13 describe a miraculous incident when the moon was intimidated into conforming with calculations of its cycle. Paragraphs 14 and 15 expand upon the second mishnaic question to the witnesses; paragraphs 16 and 17, the third; paragraph 18, the fourth. Mishnah 7 deals with the second witness and subsequent pairs. It is important to note that even though the testimony of subsequent pairs might not be necessary, they were nonetheless questioned so that they would feel good about coming and would be more inclined to do so again. This mishnaic theme of encouraging participation in the moon-witnessing process has been seen before.

2:8   Mishnah 8 describes how the head of the Bet Din declares the New Moon sanctified. Halakhah 6, paragraphs 1 through 8, discusses the sanctification of months and years, including the voting procedure. Paragraphs 9 through 11 contrast the order of voting for intercalation with the order of seating in the academy. In paragraph 11, Kahana, ordained prior to Jacob bar Aha, had been preceded by Jacob for intercalation of the year. Paragraph 12, also concerning Kahana, is a somewhat different instance of showing deference. Paragraph 13, again dealing with intercalation, tells that an old man was permitted to precede R. Simon ben Lakesh for the purpose of intercalation, even though he was not entitled. Paragraphs 14 and 15 illustrate an instance where even three cowherds were permitted to intercalate the year. Paragraphs 16 and 17 caution that the responsibility of intercalation should not be treated so lightly. Paragraph 18 picks up on the final sentence of Mishnah 8: "Rabbi Eleazar son of Rabbi Zadok says: if it is not seen in its proper time, they do not proclaim it sanctified, because heaven has already sanctified it."

2:9   The Mishnah tells how Rabban Gamaliel questioned witnesses. Then it relates an instance where he accepted seemingly impossible testimony. Halakhah 7, paragraphs 1 and 2, tells why R. Yohanan thought they were false witnesses. Paragraph 3 gives the basis for Gamaliel's acceptance of the testimony.

2:10–11   Mishnah 10 relates another instance where Rabban Gamaliel accepted seemingly impossible testimony. Here it was R. Dosa ben Harkinus who accused them of being false witnesses, with R. Joshua's agreement. In Mishnah 11, Gamaliel imposed his calendation upon R. Joshua. R. Akiba comforted Joshua that what Gamaliel had done was within his rights as the Patriarch, and could even be supported with a proof-text (Leviticus 23:4). Halakhah 8 elaborates further on the incident in Mishnah 11.

2:12   In Mishnah 12, R. Joshua went to R. Dosa ben Harkinus, his ally in Mishnah 10. R. Dosa told him that ultimately they had to accept the authority of the Patriarch and the Court, even when they were wrong! R. Joshua formally capitulated to Rabban Gamaliel. Halakhah 9, paragraphs 1 and 2, establishes by proof-text that the duly constituted court is to be obeyed, regardless of the prestige of the individual members. Paragraph 3 further relates Gamaliel's reaction to R. Joshua's capitulation. Paragraphs 4 and 5 deal with the mutual responsibility of community leaders and the people. Paragraphs 6 through 11 deal with the relationship of the solar and lunar calendars.

3:1   Mishnah 1 concludes the material on the moon-witnessing procedure. The first sentence indicates that if the Court and all Israel had seen the New Moon on the night which begins the thirtieth day, or if the witnesses had been examined but darkness intervened before the sanctification could take place, this was an intercalated month. Halakhah 1, paragraph 1, emends the Mishnah to read "either the Court or all Israel." Paragraphs 2 through 20 explore whether factors other than testimony by witnesses play a role in establishing the new month. Can visual evidence be ignored if intercalation is called for? Can sanctification take place when the New Moon has not been seen? Paragraph 9 asserts that Nisan was never intercalated and paragraph 11 says the same for Tishri, while both places affirm that it was theoretically possible. Paragraph 19 says that if they sanctified the New Moon and afterwards the witnesses were found to be lying, the sanctification is nonetheless valid. Paragraph 20 adds that "they do not minutely examine testimony with regard to the New Moon." The above-mentioned paragraphs leave the impression that at least on the stratum represented by the Gemara, mathematical calculations were probably determinant.

   The remainder of Mishnah 1 prescribes the procedure if the witnesses were themselves members of the Court. Paragraphs 21 through 28 expand upon the Mishnah. Paragraphs 29 and 30 represent two instances when two messengers sent from the Court to attest that sanctification had indeed occurred were unable to properly deliver their message. Nonetheless they were believed, suggesting that the role of the messengers was in large measure a formality.

The Shofar (3:2–4:11)

3:2   All shofars are valid except for that of a cow, because it is a "horn." Halakhah 2 examines why a cow's horn is invalid.

Mishnah 2 continues by prescribing the type, shape, and decoration of the shofar for *The New Year* (Tishri). It is to be flanked by two trumpets. The blasts are described. The first three paragraphs of Halakhah 3 deal with the shape and decoration. Paragraphs 4 and 5 deal with one's obligation to hear the blast.

3:3   Mishnah 3 prescribes the type, shape, and decoration of the shofar for fast days. Here shofars flank the trumpets. The blasts are described. Paragraph 1 of Halakhah 4 gives a midrashic explanation for the shape. Paragraphs 2 through 8 deal with required acts and liturgy for the fast day.

3:4   The Jubilee Year is equivalent to *The New Year* with regard to the blowing of the shofar and the blessings. Halakhah 5 gives the specifics.

3:5   The Mishnah deals with shofars split, in pieces, or perforated and repaired. Halakhah 6 elaborates.

3:6   The Mishnah defines what one must actually hear and do to fulfill one's obligation vis-à-vis shofar. Halakhah 7, paragraph 1, is a further comment on the need to properly direct one's heart. Paragraph 2 explores the situation of a shofar within a shofar. Paragraph 3 explores the situation of a "reversed" shofar.

3:7–8   The Mishnah contains midrashim on Exodus 17:11 and Numbers 21:8. Each midrash stresses the efficaciousness of properly directing one's heart to God. Paragraphs 1 and 2 of Halakhah 8 further embellish the midrash on Exodus 17:11, giving information about Amalek and Moses. Paragraphs 3 through 5 explain that Israel is vulnerable to the enemy as long as they forsake Torah. Halakhah 9 expands further on the midrash on Numbers 21:8 in Mishnah 8.

3:9   The Mishnah lists those whose shofar blasts do not fulfill the obligations of the community. Halakhah 10 further explores the theme.

4:1   The Mishnah deals with whether, and where, the shofar can be sounded on the Sabbath. Halakhah 1 further explores this topic.

4:2   Mishnah 2 compares Jerusalem and Yavneh with regard to sounding the shofar on the Sabbath. Halakhah 2, paragraphs 1 through 3, further defines in which towns near Jerusalem the shofar can be sounded on the Sabbath. The reason for the difference with Yavneh is explored. Paragraphs 4 and 5 further define the rules in Yavneh.

4:3   Like Mishnah 1, Mishnah 3 compares practice in the Temple with the provinces, in this case regarding *lulav*. Halakhah 3 expands upon the observance of *lulav*.

4:4   Mishnah 4, like 3, uses the formula "Originally . . . After the Temple was destroyed, Rabban Yohanan ben Zakkai decreed. . . ." This Mishnah deals with the time until which they would accept testimony. Halakhah 4 elaborates upon what happened that caused the Levites to become disordered in their singing, leading to a change in practice. It also explains what the disorder was.

4:5   Mishnah 5 includes another of Rabban Yohanan ben Zakkai's decrees. Even though Mishnah 2:7 teaches that the head of the Court announced "it is sanctified," this midrash indicates that the Court could examine witnesses in his absence.

4:6–7   These two Mishnahs give two views as to the order of the blessings for the Rosh Hashanah Additional Service. Halakhah 6 discusses local differences in practice and various liturgical versions.

4:8   The Mishnah deals with the requirements for Sovereignty, Remembrance, and Shofar Verses in the Rosh Hashanah Additional Service. Halakhah 7 elaborates.

4:9   This Mishnah specifies which leader of the services is responsible for ordering the sounding of the shofar, and which is responsible for reciting the Hallel on those occasions when it is read. Paragraphs 1, 3, 4, and 5 of Halakhah 8 explain why the Shofar Service is part of the Additional Service. Paragraph 2 explains why the Hallel is not. Paragraph 6 tells wherein the offerings for Rosh Hashanah and the Feast of Weeks are special.

4:10   The Mishnah lists restraints one must observe for the sake of the shofar, but practicing or hearing a practice blast does not fulfill one's obligation. Halakhah 9, paragraph 2, adds that adults should not prevent children from practicing shofar even on the Sabbath.

4:11   Mishnah 11 gives the rules for properly sounding the blasts, and Halakhah 10 elaborates.

I Mishnah Rosh Hashanah
Chapter One

(56a)   1. There are four New Years. On the first of Nisan is the New Year for [the reign of] kings and for [the order of] festivals. On the first of Elul is the New Year for the Tithe of Cattle; Rabbi Eleazar and Rabbi Simon say on the first of Tishri.

2. On the first of Tishri is the New Year for years, Sabbaticals, Jubilees, the young trees and vegetables. On the first of Shevat is the New Year for [fruit] trees, according to the opinion of Bet Shammai; but Bet Hillel says, on the fifteenth thereof.

3. At four times in the year the world is judged: at Passover concerning the grain, at the Festival of Weeks concerning the fruit of the tree, and on Rosh Hashanah all mortals[1] pass before Him *kivno maron*,[2] as it is said: *Who fashions the hearts of them all. Who understands all their deeds* (Psalms 33:15). And on Tabernacles they are judged concerning water.

4. On six New Moons the messengers go forth: on Nisan because of Passover, on Av because of the Fast, on Elul because of Rosh Hashanah, on Tishri because of the determination of the Festivals, on Kislev because of Chanukah, and on Adar because of Purim. And while the Temple still existed, they went forth also on Iyar because of the Minor Passover.

5. On two New Moons may the Sabbath be profaned: on Nisan and on Tishri, for on them the messengers go forth to Syria, and on them they used to determine the Festivals. And while the Temple still existed, they would profane even all of them because of the determination of the [correct time for the] sacrifice.

1. Literally, those who come into the world.
2. Explained in the Gemara.

6. Whether [the New Moon] was seen clearly or whether it was not seen clearly, they may profane the Sabbath because of it. Rabbi Jose says: if it was seen clearly, they may not profane the Sabbath because of it.

7. Once, more than forty pairs [of witnesses] were passing [through], and Rabbi Akiba detained them in Lod. Rabban Gamaliel sent to him [an admonishment]: if you detain the many, the result will be that you will cause them to stumble in the time to come.

8. If a father and a son saw the New Moon, they may [both] go [to Jerusalem to bear witness]: not because they can join with each other [to give testimony], but if one of them be found ineligible, the second may join with another. Rabbi Simon says that a father and a son, as well as all relatives, are eligible for testimony concerning the New Moon.

9. Said Rabbi Jose: once Tobiah the physician saw the New Moon in Jerusalem, he and his son and his freed slave; and the priests accepted him and his son, but declared his slave ineligible. And when they came before the Court, they accepted him and his slave, but declared his son ineligible.

10. These are ineligible [for testimony]: one who plays with dice, and a lender on interest, and pigeon-flyers, and traders in produce of the Sabbatical year, and slaves. This is the general rule: any testimony for which a woman is ineligible, also they are ineligible.

11. If one saw the New Moon but could not walk, they bring him on a donkey [on the Sabbath], or even on a litter; if any lie in wait for them, they may take staves in their hands, and if it was a long way, they may take food in their hands, since for a journey lasting a night and a day they may profane the Sabbath and go forth for testimony concerning the New Moon, as it is said: *these are the appointed seasons of the Lord, even holy convocations [which you shall proclaim in their appointed season]* (Leviticus 23:4).

Halakhah 1

Proof That Year Begins with Nisan

Gemara. 1. There are four New Years, etc. It is written: *this month [Nisan]*[3] *shall be to you the beginning of months* (Exodus 12:2).[4] *To you* [for kings and festivals][5] it shall be a beginning, but it is not a beginning for the years in general, Sabbaticals, Jubilees, the young trees[6] and vegetables.[7]

2. But I might say that *to you* it is a beginning, but it is not a beginning for [the reign of] kings or for [the order of] festivals?[8] Rabbi Jacob bar Aḥa [and] Rabbi Jose in the name of Rabbi Yoḥanan [said] it is written: *and he [Solomon] began to build [the Temple] in the second month in the second in the fourth year of his reign* (2 Chronicles 3:2). It [Scripture] paralleled *the fourth year of his reign* to *the second*[9] which refers to months. Just as we do not count *the second* which refers to the month except from Nisan, likewise we do not count *the second* which refers to *the fourth year of his reign* except from Nisan.

3. Or perhaps it is not so, but [*the second*] means the second day in the month? Wherever Scripture says *second* meaning the day of the month, it says so explicitly. Or perhaps it is not so, but [*the second*] means the second day in the week [Monday]? We have not found such dating in Scripture. But is it not written *and there was evening, and there was morning, the second day* (Genesis 1:8)? We do not derive proof from the account of the Creation of the world.[10]

4. And which *second* refers to the [order of the] months, and which *second* refers to the [month of the] year [in the reign of a

---

3. This is how the rabbis understood the scriptural text.
4. The entire verse from Ex. 12:2 is: *this month shall be to you the beginning of months, the first of the months of the year to you.*
5. *To you* is taken to show that for Jews the lunar or Jewish year begins with Nisan, which is an assumption of our Mishnah.
6. According to Lev. 19:23, the fruit of young trees was forbidden for common use during the first three years as being *orlah*. In the fourth year the fruit is redeemed, after which it could be used.
7. Deut. 14:22–29 enjoins the annual tithing of the increase of the field.
8. The exclusion implied in *to you* is total. This challenge of the claim that it is the beginning of months for kings and festivals assumes the Mishnah's affirmation.
9. This term is used twice in 2 Chr. 3:2.
10. Because there were no other divisions of time as yet.

king]?[11] Rabbi Ḥanina and Rabbi Mana [disagreed]. One said, *and he began to build in the second month*—that *second* refers to [the order of] months; *in the second*—that [the latter use of] *second* refers to the [second month of the] year [in the reign of a king]. And the other [said], even reversing the interpretation would make no difference.

5. Rabbi Simon bar Karsana in the name of Rabbi Aha derived it[12] from this: *this month shall be to you* (Exodus 12 : 2)— excluded. *It shall be the first to you*—excluded.[13] An exclusion followed by [another] exclusion [becomes an inclusion]: to include [the reign of] kings and [the order of] festivals. Then let it [the inclusion] also include the years in general, Sabbaticals, Jubilees, the young trees and vegetables?[14]

6. It is like that which Rabbi Jacob bar Aha [and] Rabbi Jose in the name of Rabbi Yoḥanan said:[15] *and he [Solomon] began to build [the Temple] in the second month in the second in the fourth year of his reign* (2 Chronicles 3 : 2). It [Scripture] paralleled *the fourth year of his reign* to *the second* which refers to months. Just as we do not count *the second* which refers to the month except from Nisan, likewise we do not count *the second* which refers to *the fourth year of his reign* except from Nisan.[16]

7. Rabbi Jonah [and] Rabbi Isaac bar Naḥman in the name of Rabbi Ḥiyya bar Joseph: *and he began to build in the second month*—that *second* refers to [the order of the] months. *In the second*—that *second* [repeated] refers to [the month in] the year [in the reign of a king]. And when it continues [with the words] *in the fourth year of his reign*, it [Scripture] paralleled *the fourth year of his reign* to *the second* which refers to [the order of the] months. Just as we do not count *the second* which refers to the month except from Nisan, likewise we do not count *the second* which refers to *the fourth year of his reign* except from Nisan.[17]

11. The word "second" appears twice in 2 Chr. 3 : 2, "in the *second* month in the *second*."

12. The assumption in the Mishnah that the first of Nisan is the New Year for kings and festivals.

13. That is, the first and second parts of the verse Ex. 12 : 2 each contain *to you* and represent exclusions.

14. Which the Mishnah assigns to the New Year that falls on the first of Tishri.

15. This passage has already been cited above in paragraph 2.

16. Chronicles, not the inclusion of Ex. 12 : 2, serves as the basis of proof.

17. This paragraph is an expansion of the paragraph immediately above and paragraph 2.

8. Samuel taught, differing:[18] *in the third month after the Is-raelites had gone forth out of the land of Egypt* (Exodus 19:1). From here [we learn] that one counts the order of the months beginning with the going forth from Egypt.[19] From this I only know months. Where do I learn years? *And the Lord spoke to Moses in the wilderness of Sinai, in [the first month of] the second year [after they had come out of the land of Egypt]* (Numbers 9:1). From this I only know that time [of the Exodus]. Where do I learn later times?[20] *In the fortieth year after the Isra-elites had come out of the land of Egypt, [in the fifth month, on the first day of the month]* (Numbers 33:38). From this I only **(56b)** know temporarily [for that generation]. Where do I learn subsequent generations? *And it was in the four hundred and eightieth year after the Israelites had come out of the land of Egypt, [in the fourth year of Solomon's reign over Israel, in the month Ziv, which is the second month, that he began to build the house of the Lord]* (1 Kings 6:1). When the Temple was built, they began to use the era from [the time of] its erection: *and it was at the end of twenty years, wherein Solomon had built the two houses, [the house of the Lord and the King's house]* (1 Kings 9:10). When they no longer merited to use the era of its erection, they began to count from its destruction: *in the twenty-fifth year of our captivity, in the beginning of the year, on the tenth day of the month,* etc. (Ezekiel 40:1). When they no longer merited to use the era of their own [events], they began to count according to the reigns of other nations:[21] *in the second year of Darius [the king, in the sixth month, on the first day of the month]* (Haggai 1:1): *in the third year of Cyrus king of Persia* (Daniel 10:1).

9. But I might say: *and he [Solomon] began to build [the Temple] in the second month in the second in the fourth year of his reign* (2 Chronicles 3:2). It [Scripture] paralleled *the fourth year of his reign* to *the second* which refers to months. Just as we do not count *the second* which refers to the month except

18. Samuel rejects the above methods for establishing Nisan as the New Year for the reign of kings and the order of festivals. He instead gathers proof-texts to illustrate change in the use of eras for chronology.

19. Since the Exodus occurred in Nisan, counting from the Exodus would also establish Nisan as the first month.

20. Those Jews who were born before the Exodus, as well as these who were born in the desert but were not part of the Exodus.

21. That is, regnal years.

from Nisan, likewise we do not count *the second* which refers to *the fourth year of his reign* except from Nisan.[22]

10. Rabbi Eleazar[23] in the name of Rabbi Ḥanina [says]: even [for dating of the regnal years of] kings of the gentile nations, one counts only from Nisan. *In the second year of Darius, in the sixth month* (Ḥaggai 1:15): *in the eighth month, in the second year of Darius* (Zechariah 1:1). [If these heathen kingdoms begin the year with Tishri], it should have said, in the eighth month, in the third year [of Darius].[24]

11. Ḥefa said *in the eighth month* (Zechariah 1:1) may have been said first,[25] for there is no necessarily implied chronological sequence in the accounts of Scripture.

12. Rabbi Jonah said, *and now, consider from this day onward—before a stone was laid [or before a stone is to be laid] upon a stone in the Temple of the Lord* (Ḥaggai 2:15).[26] How [do you chronologically order these verses from Ḥaggai and Zechariah]?[27] In the sixth month the foundation was laid;[28] in the eighth month this scriptural passage was said.[29] If you say they had already laid [stone upon stone in the ninth month], what Ḥefa said is right.[30] But if you say they did not lay [stone upon stone in the ninth month], Ḥefa said nothing.[31]

22. This passage, which already appeared in paragraphs 2 and 6 above, is repeated by Samuel to show that, although the use of eras changed, the order of the months has not, the months always beginning with Nisan.
23. The name Eleazar appears in the text with several Hebrew spellings: *Lᶜzr, Lyᶜzr, ʾLyᶜzr.*
24. The eighth month being Cheshvan, which follows Tishri. The years began with the spring equinox (Nisan) or the fall equinox (Tishri).
25. Cheshvan thus would precede Elul in the second year of Darius, which would begin with Tishri.
26. Ḥaggai 2:15–18 reads, *and now, consider from this day onward—before a stone was laid [or before a stone is to be laid] upon a stone in the Temple of the Lord . . . consider from this day onward, from the twenty-fourth day of the ninth month, from the day that the foundation of the Lord's Temple was laid, consider it.*
27. Rabbi Jonah argues that Ḥefa's statement just above necessarily implies this order:
    1. Zech. 1:1—Cheshvan (eighth month).
    2. Ḥaggai 2:15–18—Kislev (ninth month).
    3. Ḥaggai 1:15—Elul (sixth month).
If not, as in fact it is not, Ḥefa is wrong.
28. *And they came and did work in the house of the Lord of hosts, their God, on the twenty-fourth day of the month, in the sixth month, in the second year of Darius the king* (Ḥaggai 1:14–15).
29. In the eighth month Zech. 1:1 was said, and in the following month Ḥaggai 2:15–18 was said.
30. That the eighth month precedes the sixth month, and hence the New Year for dating reigns of foreign kingdoms is established in Tishri.
31. The work began in the sixth month, which preceded the ninth month.

13. Rabbi Isaac objected:[32] does it not say *and it came to pass in the six hundred and first year, in the first month, the first day of the month,*[33] *[the waters were dried up from off the earth]* (Genesis 8 : 13)?[34] And was it not taught on this verse: the year of the flood is not part of the computations [of Noah's years]?[35] This could be solved in agreement with Rabbi Eleazar's opinion, for Rabbi Eleazar has said that the world was created in Tishri.[36]

Hence Ḥefa's attempted refutation of Rabbi Eleazar in the name of Rabbi Ḥanina is meaningless, and the New Year for dating regnal years of foreign kingdoms is established in Nisan.

32. To Rabbi Ḥanina's contention that even in dating the regnal years of kings of the gentile nations, one counts from Nisan.

33. In the life of Noah.

34. Gen. 9 : 28 reads, *and Noah lived after the flood 350 years. And all the days of Noah were 950 years.* Yet according to our verse (Gen. 8 : 13), the flood ended in his 601st year, meaning that Noah lived 951 years.

35. To eliminate the contradiction between the 950 years which Noah lived and the mathematics which produce a sum of 951 years for Noah, Rabbi Isaac cites this *baraita.* The *baraita* only serves as a solution, however, if the reigns of kings are counted from Tishri. He interprets the *baraita* to mean that Noah had lived 600 years before the flood began. Hence, if Nisan were the New Year for "foreign kings," then the flood, which began on the seventeenth of Iyar, would have fallen in the 601st year of Noah's life. The following first of Nisan, which according to Gen. 8 : 13 is the day on which *the waters were dried up*, would have begun the 602nd year, not the 601st year, as our text indicates.

If Tishri is the New Year for "foreign kings," however, the calculations reconcile with Scriptures, even assuming that the Creation and the flood are figured from Nisan. Before the flood, Noah was already 600. The flood came in the eighth month of his 600th year, that is, in Iyar. The following Tishri, his 601st year began. In Nisan, still in his 601st year, the flood ended. When the *baraita* teaches that the year of the flood is not included in the number of Noah's years, it doesn't mean that the entire year of the flood can be excluded in the computation of Noah's years, but rather that the entire year of the flood is not included. Rabbi Isaac includes only up to the end of Noah's 600th year, that is, the Tishri which falls during the flood. The period of time in the 601st year is excluded because there is no longer any civilization. (This follows the interpretation of P'ne Moshe. Korban Ha'edah understands it differently.)

36. Although Rabbi Isaac has attempted to show Rabbi Ḥanina's error in dating the reigns of foreign kings from Nisan, not Tishri, both points of view appear to follow Rabbi Joshua in assuming that the world was created in Nisan. And even Rabbi Isaac's refutation of Rabbi Ḥanina is not completely successful, for the *baraita* can be understood to mean that the year of the flood is included in the 600 years of Noah's life, and the Nisan referred to in Gen. 8 : 13, the day when the waters were dried up, coincides with the beginning of Noah's 601st year. Or, if one prefers to consider the flood as additional to Noah's 600 years, the calculations of Rabbi Ḥanina still work out, since the planets did no service during the year of the flood at all (Gen. R. 25; Y. Pes. 1 27b), and therefore the year of the flood doesn't add anything to the counting of years. Hence the chronological problem can be solved as easily in agreement with Rabbi Eleazar's opinion, which would establish Tishri as the time of Creation and Cheshvan as the beginning of the flood. This is the chronology found in Seder Olam, and the *baraita* is interpreted to mean that the year of the flood does not add to Noah's years or to the years in general.

14. But is it not written: *[the words of Nehemiah the son of Hachaliah.] Now it was in the month of Kislev, in the twentieth year* (Nehemiah 1 : 1); *and it was in the month Nisan, in the twentieth year [of Artaxerxes the king]* (Nehemiah 2 : 1)?[37] This could be solved in agreement with Rabbi Eleazar's opinion, for Rabbi Eleazar has said that any year which doesn't yet have thirty days should not be classified as a complete year.[38]

15. But is it not written: *and it was the first month in the second year, on the first day of the month, that the tabernacle was reared up* (Exodus 40 : 17)? If you say that it was [in fact] the third year, [you would argue] but since it didn't yet have thirty days, they don't classify it as a complete year.

16. But is it not written: *and it was in the second year, in the second month, on the twentieth day of the month, [that the cloud was taken up from over the tabernacle of the testimony]* (Numbers 10 : 11)? And behold the year has fifty days and they did not classify it as a complete year? This is one of the challenges raised by Rabbi Isaac that remain difficult.

17. What is the [practical] difference between the one who says to count from Nisan and the one who says to count from Tishri?

18. Said Rabbi Jonah: they differ with regard to [the date of] circulating notes. Someone borrowed a loan in Iyar and wrote in it [the contract] "the second regnal year [of so and so]." Then he makes a sale [of the property under lien] in Marcheshvan and writes in it "the second regnal year [of so and so]." The authority who says we count from Nisan would date the loan prior [to the sale].[39] The one who says we count from Tishri would make the sale prior [to the loan].[40]

It is not necessary to assume that Rabbi Ḥanina is following Rabbi Joshua (the world was created in Nisan) when he says that one dates the reigns of foreign kings from Nisan also. Even believing that the world was created in Tishri, he might still date the reigns of all kings, Israelite and non-Israelite, from Nisan so as to have one chronology for all. For our text says above in paragraph 8, "when they no longer merited to count relative to [the events of] their own, they began to count according to the kingdoms [of other nations]." (This follows the interpretation of P'ne Moshe.)

37. The Hebrew MS. places the verse from Neh. 2 : 1 before the verse from Neh. 1 : 1. However, since the whole thrust of the argument is that, if the New Year for foreign kings is in Nisan, Neh. 2 : 1 should refer to the twenty-first year, I have chronologically reordered the verses in the translation.

38. Therefore even if Nisan were the New Year for foreign kings, we should not expect Neh. 2 : 1 to refer to the twenty-first year. Less than thirty days in a year are not reckoned as a year.

39. Since Iyar is the second month and Cheshvan is the eighth month.

40. Since Cheshvan is the second month and Iyar is the eighth month. The

The Use of Regnal Years in Notes

19. How [exactly do we count the reign] for kings? If he died in Adar and [another] king succeeded him in Adar, the year is attributed to the first and to the second.[41]

20. Said Rabbi Jonah: [this is so only] if [the second king's reign] extended into Nisan.[42] For if not, behold this: *[Shallum the son of Jabesh reigned in the thirty-ninth year of Uzziah King of Judah:] and he reigned a month in Samaria* (2 Kings 15 : 13).[43] You cannot interpret the years of the kings of Israel except from the years of the kings of Judah, or the years of the kings of Judah except from the years of the kings of Israel.

King David's Reign

21. It is written *and the days that David reigned over Israel were forty years, etc.* (1 Kings 2 : 11).[44] But it is also written *in Hebron he reigned over Judah seven years and six months; and in Jerusalem he reigned [thirty-three years over all Israel and Judah]* (2 Samuel 5 : 5). In the general statement they show deficit and in the particular statement they show excess?[45]

---

loan cannot be prior to the sale, because a note of indebtedness implies an obligation that the debtor's landed property is pledged to the creditor. If the debtor were to sell his property without having the money to repay his creditor, the creditor can take the property.

41. That is, documents can be dated either according to the reign of the king who died or as the first year of the new king.

42. In which case Nisan would introduce the second year of his reign.

43. In 2 Kings 15, the chronology of the rulers of Israel is given based upon the chronology of Azariah b. Amaziah, King of Judah, who ruled for fifty-two years. In the twenty-seventh year of Azariah, Jeroboam ruled Israel. Jeroboam's reign lasted until his son Zechariah replaced him in the thirty-eighth year of Azariah. Zechariah reigned only six months, and also in the thirty-eighth year of Azariah Shallum b. Jabesh began to reign. P'ne Moshe, for purposes of our discussion, assumes that Zechariah's reign lasted until the fifteenth day of Adar, and Shallum, who reigned one month, was in power from the fifteenth of Adar in Azariah's thirty-eighth year (which became Shallum's 1st year) until the fifteenth of Nisan (Azariah's thirty-ninth year, Shallum's second year). Therefore, although Shallum only reigned one month, his reign straddled two years. The fact that the thirty-ninth year of Azariah was attributed to Shallum assumes that the previous year was also attributed to him. However, had his reign begun in Adar of the thirty-eighth year but ended before Nisan introduced the thirty-ninth year of Azariah, no year would have been attributed to him.

44. The verse continues: *he reigned seven years in Hebron, and in Jerusalem he reigned thirty-three years.*

45. Both 1 Kings 2 : 11 and 2 Sam. 5 : 4 contain the general statement that David reigned forty years. The detailed enumeration in 1 Kings 2 : 11 also totals forty years; the detailed enumeration in 2 Sam. 5 : 5 totals forty years and six

22. Rabbi Isaac bar Ketsatstah[46] in the name of Rabbi Jonah [says that] there were [only] thirty-two and a half [years], but in honor of Jerusalem, Scripture rounds them off.[47] Judah Berabbi says that a larger sum absorbs a smaller sum.[48]

23. Said Rabbi Samuel bar Nahman *and when your days be filled* (2 Samuel 7 : 12).[49] The Holy One blessed be He said to him: David, I assign to you filled days;[50] I don't assign to you uncompleted days. Will not Solomon your son build the Temple only to offer sacrifices [therein]?[51] Your justice and righteousness are more dear to me than all the sacrifices, as it is written: *to do righteousness and justice is more acceptable to the Lord than sacrifice* (Proverbs 21 : 3).[52]

24. Rav Huna said, all those six months during which David was fleeing from Absalom his son, he was making atonement offerings with a she-goat, like a commoner.[53]

---

months. Hence general statements indicating forty years to David's reign are short six months of the total in 2 Sam.

46. A questionable name which does not appear elsewhere in this form.

47. The detailed enumeration in 2 Sam. is not exact. After David's reign of seven years six months in Hebron, he ruled thirty-two and a half years in Jerusalem. The total, forty years, is thus correct. The confusion enters in because the thirty-two and a half was rounded off to thirty-three in honor of Jerusalem.

48. The detailed enumeration in 2 Sam. is correct, but the forty and a half years have been rounded off to forty. According to Jastrow (p. 189), "Berabbi" is a "title of scholars, most frequently applied to disciples of R. Judah Hanasi and his contemporaries, but also to some of his predecessors, and sometimes to the first Amoraim."

49. That is, rounded off.

50. According to Psalms 90 : 10, *the days of our years are seventy years, or even by reason of strength eighty years.* David lived seventy years, and therefore he fulfilled his days.

According to Seder Olam Rabbah, chapter 13, p. 29a, line 8 (Ratner edition), David was twenty-nine years old when he was anointed by Samuel. 2 Sam. 5 : 4 relates that David was thirty years old when all the elders of Israel came together to Hebron to anoint David king. Hence either the total of forty or forty and a half years would be correct for the length of David's reign, depending on which anointment one counts from.

51. The translation follows the reading in the parallel passages: *klum Shlomo binkhah.*

52. And hence David's allotted days were fulfilled, even though this prolongation postponed the construction of the Temple.

53. Lev. 4 : 22–23 commands: *when a ruler sins and does through error any ne of all the things which the Lord his God has commanded not to be done, and s guilty; if his sin, wherein he has sinned, be known to him, he shall bring for his offering a goat, a male without blemish.* If David was "a ruler" during this six-month period, he was obligated to bring only he-goats as sin offerings. If instead he brought she-goats, the sin-offerings of the common people (Lev. 4 : 27–29), he could not have considered himself a ruler, and therefore the six months during which he fled from his son Absalom (2 Sam. 15 : 13–18 : 15) were not included in his reign and he ruled forty years.

25. Said Rabbi Judah the son of Rabbi Shalom: it is written, *For six months Joab remained there with all Israel, [until he had cut off every male in Edom]* (1 Kings 11:16). [He explained it:] the Holy One blessed be He said to him, I have said to you, *meddle not with them* (Deuteronomy 2:5).[54] But you did meddle with them. Therefore, by your life, they [these six months] are not attributed to you![55]

The New Year of the Festival

26. Who is the authority for [the statement concerning] festivals?[56] It is Rabbi Simon. For Rabbi Simon said,[57] the three festivals must follow consecutively [for a full year], except that Passover always must be first. You find that he said, sometimes five [festivals constitute the required full year], sometimes four, sometimes three. [If he vows] before the Festival of Weeks—five. Before Tabernacles—four. Before Passover—three.[58] Rabbi Eleazar the son of Rabbi Simon said: only Passover must be last. Consequently, sometimes three, sometimes two, sometimes one.[59] But the Sages say that the festival which he [first] encounters shall be first, but all [three] festivals of the year always must pass [before he violates the vow].

27. It is written: *besides the Sabbaths of the Lord, and besides your gifts, etc.* (Leviticus 23:38).[60] *Which you shall give to the Lord* (Leviticus 23:38). What is Scripture saying? You might

54. The Edomites. The verse continues: *for I will not give you of their land, no, not so much as a foot breadth; because I have given Mount Seir to Esau for a possession.*

55. Leaving an even forty years. Joab was captain of the host for David, and this text refers to the six months when David was in Edom.

56. Our Mishnah states that Passover is the New Year for festivals, i.e., we count from Passover with regard to lateness of vows.

57. In Tosefta Rosh Hashanah 1:2.

58. The text is more complete in b. R.H. 4a. The underlying legal question has to do with the means of determining when someone who makes a vow has transgressed the precept in Deut. 23:22: *when you vow a vow to the Lord your God, you shall not delay to pay it.* Rabbi Simon's position is that a transgression has occurred if the one who vows allows three consecutive festivals, beginning with Passover, to pass before he has paid. Hence, if he vows between Tabernacles and Passover, three consecutive festivals must pass before he is culpable for transgressing *you shall not delay*; between Passover and the Festival of Weeks, five; between the Festival of Weeks and Tabernacles, four.

59. If he vows before the Festival of Weeks, all three must pass, with Passover the third; before Tabernacles, two; before Passover, he must also pay during Passover or transgress.

60. The verse continues: *and besides all your vows, and besides all of your gift offerings which you shall give to the Lord.*

think that on a festival only the sacrifices of that festival alone may be brought. Whence do you know that the sacrifices offered by individuals and that the congregational sacrifices, whether they be consecrated on the festival or before the festival, may be brought [as an offering] on the festival?[61] Scripture says, *besides the Sabbaths of the Lord . . .* (Leviticus 23:38). *Which you shall give to the Lord* (Leviticus 23:38). These refer to the birds and the meal offerings—to include all of them that are offered on a festival. One might think that this refers to optional offerings? Therefore Scripture says *these things you shall do for the Lord in your set festivals [besides your vows, and your gift offerings . . .]* (Numbers 29:39). *These [things you shall do]* establishes them as obligatory, that all of them shall be offered on the festival. One might think: on whatever festival one wishes? Therefore Scripture says *and you shall come there. And you shall bring there [your burnt offerings, and your sacrifices, and your tithes, and heave offerings of your hand, and your vows, and your gift offerings . . .]* (Deuteronomy 12:5–6). If [the purpose of the verse were only] to grant permission, Scripture has already permitted [by verse cited above].[62] If [the purpose of the verse is] to set the time, this too is already established [by verse cited above].[63] If so, why does Scripture say *and you shall come there, and you shall bring* there . . . (Deuteronomy 12:5–6)? It is [to teach that] this [refers to the] first festival [of the three] you encounter [after the vow].[64]

28. One might think that if one of [the festivals] passes and the offering was not brought, this would constitute transgression of *you shall not delay [to pay it]?* Therefore Scripture says, *these things shall you do for the Lord in your set festivals* (Numbers 29:39).[65] One does not transgress *you shall not delay* until all the festivals of the year pass.

29. Rabbi Simon says, the three festivals must follow consecutively. How? If one vows before Passover, [a transgression is not effected] until Passover and the Festival of Weeks and Tabernacles pass. If he vows before the Festival of Weeks, until the

61. During *Hol Hamoed*, the intermediate, or nonsacred, days of the festival.
62. Lev. 23:38.
63. Num. 29:39.
64. Hence this follows the position of the Sages stated at the end of the previous paragraph.
65. "Festivals" is plural.

Festival of Weeks and Tabernacles and Passover and the Festival of Weeks and Tabernacles pass.[66] If he vows before Tabernacles, until Tabernacles and Passover and the Festival of Weeks and Tabernacles pass.

(56c)   30. The question was raised before Rabbi Ila, so far [we know] a positive injunction [has been transgressed];[67] how do we know also a negative prohibition?[68] Scripture says *and you shall come there, and you shall bring there* (Deuteronomy 12 : 5–6).[69] With what are we dealing? If it be a positive injunction [to bring payment by the first festival], it was already said elsewhere;[70] but since it is not a matter of positive injunction, you must interpret it as a matter of negative prohibition.[71]

31. The paschal sacrifice, which was set to be sacrificed at the proper time, [if he did not do so] does he transgress?[72] You find that it is taught: Passover sacrifices [neglected] in their time constitute transgression.[73] For if it is not so, what are we saying? Said Rabbi Samuel the son of Rabbi Jose the son of Rabbi Abun: [the *baraita* is necessary] so that you will not say that if it [the lamb] is lost and it is found after the owners had their atonement [by another paschal lamb as a substitute], it [the first] will be sacrificed as a peace-offering;[74] therefore it is [still] necessary

66. In Tosefta Rosh Hashanah 1 : 2, and above in paragraph 26, Rabbi Simon said "the three festivals must follow consecutively [for a full year], except that Passover always must be first."

67. Deut. 23 : 24: *that which has gone out of your lips you shall observe and do.*

68. Not to come to the Temple on the festival without bringing your vows.

69. That is, each time you come, bring your vows.

70. Num. 29 : 39: *these things you shall do for the Lord in your set festivals. . . .*

71. See note 68 above.

72. Is the paschal lamb, like the other cases of "you shall not delay," considered late only after three festivals have passed? Or, since it has a fixed date of the fourteenth of Nisan, is it unacceptable once the festival has passed? For it seems paradoxical to say that one may wait three festivals to do the paschal offering. Tosefta Arachin 3 : 17 has an answer to the question: "Those who are liable for burnt-offerings, a money valuation, peace-offerings, a valuation, a ḥerem, consecrations, vows, gift offerings, sin-offerings, trespass-offerings, charity contributions, tithes, gleanings, forgotten sheaves and corners of the field, firstborn, tithe of cattle, *paschal lamb*, as soon as three festivals have passed, they transgress the negative prohibition of 'you shall not delay.'"

73. That is, if the paschal offering is not made during its fixed time, the negative prohibition of "you shall not delay" is immediately transgressed.

74. Mishnah Pesachim 9 : 6 deals with the Passover offering lost before Passover and subsequently found either before or after the festival. If it is late, the newly found lamb can no longer serve as the paschal offering, but rather it be-

[to pose the original question:] the paschal sacrifice, which was set to be sacrificed at the proper time, [if he did not do so] does he transgress?[75]

32. The question was raised before Rabbi Zeira: [if one who has vowed goes to Jerusalem] in the interval between one festival and the other, [if he did not bring his offering] does he transgress?[76] Replied Rabbi Abba, and has it not been taught: a *chagigah* that was not sacrificed on the first [festival] should be sacrificed on the second?[77] And would they permit him to transgress [day by day]![78]

33. And furthermore it[79] can be derived from this: *you shall do*—the positive injunction; *you shall observe*—the negative prohibition (Deuteronomy 23:24).[80] But does he transgress a positive injunction and a negative prohibition unless three festivals passed him [since his vow]?

34. Rabbi Abun, in the name of the rabbis from there [Babylonia]: concerning the one who vows, "be a burnt offering obligatory upon me to bring on Monday," if Monday passes and he has not brought it, he transgresses.

If its[81] year ends, you throw [at him the possibility of fulfilling the vow] the last day [prior to its being one year old] and [thereafter] he transgresses for each day. If this is so, when three festivals have passed [since one made a vow], you throw [at him the possibility of fulfilling the vow] at the last festival [of the three] and [thereafter] he transgresses for each festival.

35. Rabbi Abun bar Ḥiyya asked: if its[81] year ends on the

comes a peace-offering after Passover. Rabbi Samuel understands the *baraita* to teach that, although you might think the newly recovered lamb is to be treated as a peace-offering and hence considered in violation of "you shall not delay" only after three festivals have passed, in fact it is treated as a paschal offering and hence violates the negative prohibition immediately upon lateness.

75. The original question still stands: if he does not bring the paschal offering at the proper time, is he violating "you shall not delay"?

76. Deut. 12:5–6: *and you shall come there, and you shall bring there.* This is interpreted in paragraph 30 above as the negative injunction not to come to the Temple on the festival without bringing your vows.

77. And not before, that is, not during the intermediate days.

78. Hence, even if he goes up to Jerusalem between festivals, the obligation learned from Deut. 12:5–6, "and you shall come there, and you shall bring there," applies only on the festival itself.

79. The ruling in the paragraph above with regard to the intervals between festivals.

80. Deut. 23:24 reads: *that which has gone out of your lips you shall observe and do.*

81. The animal's, such as a lamb.

Festival of Weeks, is it possible to say that it is not fit [as a gift offering on the festival] and [yet] he transgresses?[82] It follows this: *the fat of my feast shall not remain all night until the morning* (Exodus 23:18). But may the *emurim* of the weekday be offered on a festival?[83] Said Rabbi Abbahu, I interpret that opinion for a case when the fourteenth falls on the Sabbath.[84] Rabbi Jonah[85] asked, but if the fourteenth falls on the Sabbath, a *chagigah* doesn't come with it![86] Scripture means that they offered it when it was still day[87] so as not to transgress *[the fat of my feast] shall not remain all night until the morning* (Exodus 23:18). And here they also offered it when it was still day [on the day before the festival] so as not to transgress "you shall not delay [to pay it"] (Deuteronomy 23:22). Said Rabbi Hin'na, if he transgressed and brought [the offering on the Festival itself], would it not be fit; since if he would have transgressed and brought [it], it would have been fit. [Therefore, since he didn't,] he transgresses.[88]

36. It is written: *you shall eat it before the Lord your God year by year* (Deuteronomy 15:20). A year for it, and a year for its substitute; a year for the unblemished, and a year for the blemished; a year for the first-born and a year for sacrifices. "Year by year" teaches that the first-born is eaten for two days and two years![89] How can this be? You may slaughter it on Rosh

82. That is, he is forced into lateness through the prohibition against carrying out the sacrifice on a festival.

83. The *emurim* are those portions of sacrifices offered on the altar. In this case, *emurei chagigah* refers to the *emurim* of the pilgrim's feast offering. According to the verse from Ex. 23:18, the fat of the animal slaughtered on the fourteenth of Nisan must be offered before the morning of the fifteenth, and hence must be offered during the night of the festival!

84. In which case the fats of the Sabbath would be offered on the night of the festival. Hence the application of Ex. 23:18 is limited to the case where the fourteenth of Nisan falls on the Sabbath.

85. Although no authority is cited in connection with this question in the Leiden MS of Rosh Hashanah, Rabbi Jonah asks it in the parallel passage from Pesachim in the Leiden MS. In the genizah parallel passage of Rosh Hashanah, the authority cited is Rabbi Jose.

86. Pesachim 6:3. The *chagigah* offering supplemented, if necessary, the meal on the night of Passover. Yet unlike the Passover offering, the slaughtering of the *chagigah* does not override the Sabbath. Hence, how can Rabbi Abbahu apply Ex. 23:18 to the fourteenth?

87. On the day before Passover when the fourteenth was not a Sabbath.

88. "You shall not delay."

89. Parallel passage is in b. Bekorot 27b. The text "year by year" denotes one day in this year and one day in the next year.

Hashanah eve and eat it on Rosh Hashanah eve and on Rosh Hashanah.[90]

37. Rabbi Ishmael taught: if fifteen days from the end of its year it received a blemish, it may be kept alive after the year until the fifteenth day.[91] Said Rabbi Ila: it follows that the year of the blemished animal is not clear [from the Torah].

38. Said Rabbi Jose: a *baraita* supports Rabbi Ila. With regard to the firstling at this time,[92] may it not be kept alive even four or five years before yet showing it to an expert? How do we interpret it?[93] If with regard to an unblemished animal, isn't it already said? But since it is not a matter of the unblemished animal, make it a matter of the blemished animal.

39. [The rule] both for a firstling and for all consecrated animals is that one transgresses[94] with regard to them from the point where [they have been kept three] festivals [even if] less than a year, or a year [even] without [three] festivals. I grant that [three] festivals without a year [are possible]; but how is a year [possible] without [three] festivals?[95] There [in Babylonia] they say: it may be solved that it was deficient in time at Passover.[96] But it is said there that the [animal which is] suitable for a part of the year is suitable for all of it. Say also here that the [animal which is] suitable for a part of the Passover is suitable for all of it.[97] Said Rabbi Abba Mari: it may be solved in the case where the Festival of Weeks falls on the fifth [of Sivan], the animal is born the sixth, [and the following year] the Festival of Weeks falls on the seventh.[98]

90. That is, slaughter it before sunset on the last day of Elul, and eat it before sunset as well as after. Hence it is being eaten in the old and new year.
91. Therefore it may be kept alive a total of thirty days from the time it received a blemish. This is true in any instance where the blemish is received within its year.
92. When sacrifices are no longer made.
93. With what case is this *baraita* dealing?
94. The precept of not delaying.
95. See b. R.H. 6b for discussion.
96. That is, it was not yet eight days old. According to Lev. 22:27, the animal is only acceptable for an offering made by fire to the Lord when it is eight days old or more. Since it was not yet of age, this festival was not attributed to it, resulting in a year without three festivals.
97. That is to say, even if the animal was too young to be sacrificed, the festival should be attributed to it. For in the case of an animal for sacrifice, the animal is sanctified from birth even though it is only sacrificed at the due time. And here, the animal which has not yet reached the age of eight days on the first day of Passover will nonetheless achieve the age of eight days before the seventh day of Passover is over.
98. If Nisan and Iyar both have thirty days in the regulated calendar, the Fes-

40. Rabbi Abun bar Ḥiyya asked before Rabbi Zeira: it is written *he shall not inquire whether it be good or bad* (Leviticus 27 : 33).[99] If he violated and did inquire, does he transgress? He said to him, every matter [of injunction] that is intended to be permissive, one does not transgress.[100] What does it [the injunction] come to permit here? Scripture sanctions to dedicate [i.e. to tithe] blemished animals.

41. Elsewhere[101] we learn, "on the eighth day he [the leper] brought three beasts: a sin-offering, a guilt-offering, and a burnt-offering; and a poor man brought a sin-offering of a bird and a burnt-offering of a bird."[102] But is not the [poor man's] sin-offering of a bird deficient in time relative to the guilt-offering?[103] Said Rabbi Eleazar: here Scripture sanctions to dedicate [animals] deficient in time.

42. Rabbi Abba bar Mammal asked before Rabbi Ami: it is written *and on the eighth day he shall bring [two turtle-doves, or two young pigeons, to the priest . . .]* (Numbers 6 : 10).[104] If he violated and didn't bring them, does he transgress?[105] He said to him, every matter [injunction] that is intended to be permissive, one does not transgress. What does it [the injunction] come to permit? It is like that which Rabbi Eleazar said [with regard to the leper]: here Scripture sanctions to dedicate [animals] deficient in time.

43. Said Rabbi Jose the son of Rabbi Abun: all [the first] seven [days of the nazarite], we[106] do not require him to bring [the offerings]; only from this point on [the eighth day] do we require him to bring. A *baraita* contradicts Rabbi Jose the son of

tival of Weeks would occur on the fifth of Sivan, this being the fiftieth day from the second day of Passover.

99. The reference is to the tithe of the herd or flock. One should not select the tithe, whether proper or defective. The question is whether the verse is injunctive or permissive.

100. If he acts with greater stringency.

101. Mishnah Nega'im 14 : 7.

102. For a guilt-offering, however, he must also bring a beast at a later time.

103. In Mishnah Zevachim 10 : 5 it says, "all sin-offerings in the Torah precede guilt-offerings, except a leper's guilt-offering, because it comes to make [a person] fit [to enter the Temple and partake of sacrifices]." So here he should have brought a guilt-offering first, but he postponed this offering.

104. The reference is to the nazarite in the case where someone died suddenly in his presence, causing him to be in a state of defilement. To remove this uncleanness, he cut off his hair on the seventh day and brought his offerings on the eighth day.

105. You shall not delay.

106. I.e., the Bet Din.

Rabbi Abun: all of them plan and bring their offerings on the [next] festival.[107] This is right for the nazarite,[108] but the leper, is he not wanting [the ceremony of] atonement [for full restoration to cleanness]?[109] For do we not learn, "the [recital of the whole] Hallel and the rejoicing [continued for] eight days"?[110] Solve it by [saying that it refers to] the nazarite [only].[111]

44. Rabbi Zechariah, the son-in-law of Rabbi Levi, asked: the beginning [of the *baraita*][112] you interpret to refer to the nazarite and the end to the leper? Said Rabbi Ḥananiah the son of Rabbi Hillel, was [that difficulty] not raised[113] elsewhere?[114] And Rabbi Jose said that Rabbi Eudemus Neḥota[115] interpreted

107. The reference is to Moed Katan 3:1. There the Mishnah enumerates all those who may shave their hair during the festival week. Included is the nazarite emerging from the state of ritual impurity which resulted from contact with a corpse and the leper emerging from his state of impurity.

108. Unlike a leper, a nazarite may rejoice from the beginning of the festival, even though he has not yet made his offering.

109. Until such time as he has atoned through his offering, he cannot touch sanctified objects and hence cannot partake of the festival offerings. He cannot make his offering on the first day of the festival, and therefore he cannot fulfill Mishnah Sukah 4:1, to rejoice, i.e., eating meat, for eight days.

110. Mishnah Sukah 4:1. Rejoicing means the consumption of peace-offerings (Deut. 16:14; b. Pesachim 109a).

111. And that the possibility of applying the word *shmoneh*—rejoicing for eight days—does not apply to the leper.

112. The *baraita* referred to is "all of them plan [from the eighth day]. . . ." P'ne Moshe emends the text to read: "the beginning you explain with the leper and the end with the nazarite?" The assumption in making the emendation which exchanges "leper" and "nazarite" is that the phrase "all of them" in the *baraita* means all those enumerated in Moed Katan 3:1, and that would include the leper. Following this emendation, Rabbi Zechariah is questioning whether the second part of the *baraita*, "but they bring their offerings on the next festival," can exclude the leper yet apply to the nazarite.

113. The question being asked is whether in fact the eight days of rejoicing described in Mishnah Sukah 4:1, include everyone in the obligation, or whether the leper, who cannot sacrifice on the first day if he has not yet been fully restored to cleanness, can be excluded from this obligation. Mitigating against such exclusion is the fact that our Mishnah teaches "[the ceremonials of] the *lulav* and the willow [continued for] six [days] or seven." This variation depends upon when the Sabbath falls, and hence provides for special circumstances. With regard to the rejoicing, however, the Mishnah does not say "seven days or eight."

Rabbi Ḥananiah the son of Rabbi Hillel supports the exclusion of the leper from the obligation to rejoice for eight days. He does so by showing that when the first day of the festival falls on Sabbath, the he-goats of the festival are eaten raw by the priests, but the peace-offerings do not supersede the Sabbath and hence people are excluded from rejoicing for eight days. So here likewise the leper can be excluded from rejoicing for eight days, the obligation for rejoicing for eight days lying only with the priests.

114. In Y. Sukah 4, Halakhah 5.

115. In the Jastrow dictionary, p. 894, "Neḥota" is translated as "who had been in Babylonia." In Frankel's *Introduction to the Yerushalmi*, on p. 60a, he says that Eudemus was named Neḥota because he regularly went to Babylonia.

as follows: with regard to the priests and the he-goats. So also here, the priests with he-goats.

45. Rabbi Ḥaggai asked before Rabbi Jose: it is written *and on the eighth day [the flesh of his foreskin] shall be circumcised* (Leviticus 12:3). [What happens if] he transgressed and didn't circumcise?[116] He [Rabbi Jose] said to him: *when you shall vow a vow to the Lord your God, you shall not delay to* **pay** *it* (Deuteronomy 23:22). A matter subject to payments; it exempts this case which is not subject to payments.

46. *You shall not delay to pay* **it**,[117] and not its substitute, as it is taught *and to the door of the tent of meeting has not brought* **it** (Leviticus 17:4), and not its substitute.

47. Said Rabbi Jonah, Levi ben Sisi interpreted it[118] before Rabbi: concerning the one who says "I obligate myself to a burnt-offering" and three festivals pass and he brings another [a substitute] and offers it immediately, I would have said that he is exempted from [the obligation of] the first one. Therefore it is necessary to say *you shall not delay to pay* **it**, and not its substitute.

48. Said Rabbi Jose, [but if this is] with regard to the one who says "I obligate myself," [since it is a vow,] he transgresses immediately! Rather this is the case before us: concerning the one who says, "this shall be a burnt-offering," and two festivals pass, and he brings another [a substitute] in its stead and he doesn't offer it immediately, and the third festival passes, I would have said that you should count [the original] with a substitute [to total] three festivals. Therefore it is necessary to say *you shall not delay to pay* **it**, and not its substitute.

49. *For he will surely require it*:[119] these refer to sin-offerings and guilt-offerings.[120] *The Lord your God*: this refers to an object dedicated for keeping the Temple in repair.[121] *Of you*: that

116. Did he transgress "you shall not delay"?
117. Commentaries note the fact that Scripture reads "to pay *it*" rather than simply "to pay," thus excluding the possibility of a substitute should the animal suffer a blemish after being consecrated.
118. And not its substitute.
119. Our text takes Deut. 23:22 and expounds it phrase by phrase. The verse reads, *for the Lord your God will surely require it of you; and it will be sin in you.*
120. The term "require" indicates that the vow and gift offerings are not the subject of the second half of the verse, since they could not be required.
121. Since this phrase appears in the first half of the verse and hence seems superfluous in the second half, it can be expounded to indicate that also things dedicated to God, not only things dedicated to the priesthood or altar, require prompt payment.

is, gleanings, forgotten sheaves, and corners of the field.[122] *And it will be sin in you*: but not sin in your offering.[123] For if it is not so, what do we mean?[124]

50. Said Rabbi Samuel the son of Rabbi Jose the son of Rabbi Abun: so that you will not say, perhaps the sacrifice will be found unfit,[125] therefore it is necessary to say, *and it will be sin in you*, but not sin in your offering.[126]

51. *That which has gone out of your lips you shall observe and do* (Deuteronomy 23:24). *You shall observe and do*—to warn the Bet Din that they shall make you [observe and do]. The Rabbis of Caesarea in the name of Rabbi Abuna: from here [we learn that one is subject to offer] a pledge [for fulfillment of a vow].[127] *According as you have vowed to the Lord your God a gift* (Deuteronomy 23:24). And is there a "vow" which is called a "gift"?[128] But [this verse comes rather] to make liable [on you shall not delay] for every vow and every gift offering [separately].

52. What is [the formula of] that which they designated as a vow? When one says, "I obligate myself to a burnt-offering." And what is [the formula of] that which they designated as a gift? When one says, "this shall be a burnt-offering."

53. Rabbi Ḥama, the Fellow of the [Council of] Rabbis,[129] asked what if he said "I obligate myself"[130] and repented and said "this shall be . . ."?[131] Rabbi Hin'na asked [challenging the question]: this is not logical if he did not say "this shall be . . ." and repented and said "I obligate myself."[132] A more stringent

---

122. The commentators suggest that *of you* indicates "gleanings, forgotten sheaves, and corners of the field," which are left for the poor, because of the wording found in Ex. 22:24, . . . *the poor who is in your power*, i.e., *of you*. Here the Hebrew word being commented upon is the same, meaning *of you*.

123. That is, you have sinned by your lateness, but the animal is not thereby unfit.

124. If the scriptural verse does not mean to exclude disqualification of the animal through lateness by the term "in you," what could it mean?

125. If made late.

126. I have followed the reading suggested by an editor of the MS.

127. In Mishnah Arachin 5:6 we read: "Pledges must be taken from them that are bound by a vow of valuation, but from them that are liable to sin-offerings or guilt-offerings pledges are not taken. A pledge must be taken from those who owe burnt-offerings or peace-offerings. . . ."

128. The rabbis find this scriptural usage where a "gift-offering" is "vowed" to be strange, since the gift-offering (*ndavah*) and the vow (*neder*) constitute two separate categories.

129. This is Jastrow's rendering of *ḥaber*. Other possible translations exist, such as "scholar," "fellow student," "member of an order."

130. The formula for a vow-offering.

131. The formula for a gift-offering.

132. That is, the question raised by R. Ḥama makes no sense if the formula for the vow-offering precedes the formula for the gift-offering, since the more

(56d)   prohibition takes precedence over a less stringent prohibition;
but a less stringent prohibition doesn't take precedence over a
more stringent prohibition.

54. They [the Rabbis] have added to them[133] the payment of
rent and the offering of the shekel. The payment of rent: said
Rabbi Jonah, only if [the renter] said "[rent] for this year," but if
he said "one year," he rents it from one point of time to the
other.[134]

55. And the offering of the shekel: like that which Rabbi
Samuel bar Isaac said,[135] as [the time of] its beginning, *and it
came to pass in the first month in the second year, on the first
day of the month, that the tabernacle was reared up* (Exodus
40 : 17). And it is taught concerning it: on the day that the tabernacle was reared up, on that very day the offering was taken
[from the treasury].[136]

56. Rabbi Tabi [and] Rabbi Josiah in the name of Kahana: it
is written here .. . *the months of [the year]* (Numbers 28 : 14)
and it is written elsewhere . . . *the months of [the year]* (Exodus
12 : 2). Just as elsewhere the use of *the months of* is counted only
from Nisan, so *the months of* here is counted only from Nisan.

57. Said Rabbi Jonah: Rabbi Tabi left out the first part [of
the *baraita*] and cited [only] the end. But it is not so![137] It should
be taught thusly: *this is the burnt-offering of the new moon in
its month* (Numbers 28 : 14). It might be said that he would be
obligated to offer *T'rumah* every month? Therefore Scriptures
says *in **its** month of the months*. He offers one *T'rumah* for all
the months of the year. It might be [that he would offer it] in
whatever month he wishes? It is written here . . . *the months of*

---

stringent vow-offering, which requires a surety against nonpayment, cannot be
voided in favor of the less stringent gift-offering. Therefore Rabbi Hin'na argues
that "this shall be" must have preceded "I obligate myself," and therefore the
more stringent vow-offering superseded the less stringent gift-offering.

133. To items listed in the Mishnah where the New Year falls on the first of
Nisan.

134. The difference between the vow "this year" and "one year" is discussed
in Nedarim 8 : 1. If one vows "this year," the beginning of the following year
belongs to the future. If one vows "one year," he obligates himself for a full year
of days, that is, from that day until the same date and month a year hence.

135. In Y. Shekalim 1, Halakhah 1.

136. I.e., all of the shekels which were collected during the campaign.

137. What he has given us of the *baraita* does not suffice to establish Nisan as
the New Year for the contribution of the shekel. For the verse as a whole can be
read, "this is the burnt-offering of the new moon in its month throughout the
months of the year." From what Rabbi Tabi has given us, we don't know how to
understand *the months of the year* in Num. 28 : 14. The rest of the *baraita* clarifies this problem. The argument is better understood from the parallel passage in
b. R.H. 7a.

[the year] (Numbers 28:14) and it is written elsewhere . . . *the months of [the year]* (Exodus 12:2). Just as elsewhere the use of *the months of* is counted only from Nisan, so *the months of* here is counted only from Nisan.

58. [138] Elsewhere[139] we have learned: Rabbi Meir says: on the first of Elul it is the New Year for the tithe of cattle.[140] Ben Azzai says: those born in Elul are tithed by themselves.[141]

59. Rav Huna said this is the reasoning of Rabbi Meir: up to that time [the first of Elul] the latest births of the old year [of those conceived before the first of Nisan] take place; beyond that time they begin to give birth from the new ones [conceived after the first of Nisan].

60. Rabbi Jose the son of Rabbi Abun in the name of Rav Huna [said] the reasoning of Rabbi Eleazar and Rabbi Simon:[142] *the rams have mounted the sheep* (Psalms 65:14). Those refer to the early-bearing sheep. *The valleys also are covered over with offspring* (ibid.). Those refer to the sheep which conceive late in the season. *They pasture and are tithed* (ibid.). These [born early] and those [born late] enter into the shed to be tithed.[143]

61. Said Ben Azzai: since some say thus and others say otherwise, let those [the sheep] born in Elul be tithed by themselves.[144] How is this? If he has five born in Av, five in Elul, and

138. The Gemara is now interpreting the next clause of our Mishnah.
139. In Mishnah Bechorot 9:5.
140. In the parallel text of the printed Y. Shekalim 3, Halakhah 1, the reading is: Rabbi Meir says: the first of Elul is the New Year for the tithe of cattle. Rabbi Eleazar and Rabbi Simon say, on the first of Tishri. Ben Azzai says: those born in Elul are tithed by themselves. Mishnah Bechorot 9:5 agrees with the MS version.
141. And neither with those born in Av nor with those born in Tishri, as there is a doubt whether the New Year for tithing is the first of Tishri or the first of Elul.
142. In Mishnah R.H. 1:1, where it says: Rabbi Eleazar and Rabbi Simon say the first of Tishri [is the New Year for tithing cattle].
143. Rabbi Eleazar and Rabbi Simon have made a midrash on Psalms 65:14: *the meadows are clothed with flocks; the valleys also are covered over with corn; they shout for joy, yea, they sing.* The midrash can be made because the word *kar* means "ram" as well as "meadow"; *bar* means "offspring" as well as "grain." From the root *resh vav ayin* comes the meaning "to shout" and also "to pasture." The roots meaning "to sing" (*shin yod resh*) and "to tithe" (*ayin shin resh*) share two of three letters and are hence closely enough related to suggest this midrash: *yasheru* is read as if it were *ya'sheru.*
Rabbi Eleazar and Rabbi Simon also take the verse more literally in determining when the sheep which conceive late in the season will give birth. If they conceive when the valleys are covered with corn, this is Nisan. Hence they would bear in Elul, and the New Year which would permit for the tithing in the same year of those conceived both early and late would be Tishri. The tithing period would therefore end on the last day of Elul.
144. Rabbi Meir says the first of Elul. Rabbi Eleazar and Rabbi Simon say the

five in Tishri, they do not combine. But if he has five born in Av and five in Tishri, they combine.[145]

62. And would Ben Azzai arbitrate the views of his disciples?[146] Rabbi Jeremiah [and] Rabbi Mesha in the name of Rabbi Samuel bar Rav Isaac: for the fathers of the world differed about it.

63. Who are "the fathers of the world"? Rabbi Jonah in the presence of Rabbi Jeremiah teaches: Rabbi Ishmael and Rabbi Akiba. It follows from this that Ben Azzai was both a pupil and a colleague to Rabbi Akiba. For if you say [Rabbi Akiba was only] his teacher, is there a person who says to his teacher "since some say thus and others say otherwise . . ."?

64. Rabbi Abbahu in the name of Rabbi Samuel the son of Rav Isaac learned it from this:[147] Ben Azzai said to him [Rabbi Akiba], we [already] grieve over those things concerning which they differ, but you have come to bring us dissension over that concerning which they agree. It follows that Ben Azzai was a colleague and a pupil to Rabbi Akiba. For if you say [Rabbi Akiba was only] his teacher, is there a person who says to his teacher: you have come to bring dissension[148] [upon us]?[149]

65. Elsewhere[150] we learn: [all animals born] from the first of Tishri to the twenty-ninth of Elul combine [for the tithe of cattle]. Five born before Rosh Hashanah and five born after Rosh Hashanah do not combine. But five born before the period [of tithing] and five born after the period [of tithing] do combine [to enter the same shed for tithing].[151]

66. If so, why did they speak of three periods[152] for the tithing of cattle? [It is for the purpose of informing us that] until the

---

first of Tishri. Since the division between years is not clear, we cannot chance tithing the old with the new, so we tithe those born in Elul by themselves.

145. In this case, Av follows Tishri in the same year.

146. Rabbi Meir, Rabbi Simon, Rabbi Eleazar flourished a generation after Ben Azzai.

147. Mishnah Baba Batra 9 : 10. Proof that Ben Azzai was a pupil-colleague.

148. The context of the quotation from Baba Batra shows Bet Hillel and Bet Shammai in apparent agreement. The question therefore asked is that, if Bet Hillel and Bet Shammai seem to agree, why should Rabbi Akiba introduce a note of discord by asserting that even here they are in dispute?

149. "Upon us" follows the reading from parallel passage in Shekalim.

150. In Mishnah Bechorot 9 : 6.

151. That is, it is possible to tithe the animals born after a tithing period for animals born before it. This is not so in the case of the New Year for tithing animals, whereby animals born after it cannot be tithed for those born before it.

152. Literally, threshing floors. The threshing floor is the place where the grain is to be made fit for food and where it is made subject to tithes. Similarly, the respective periods of tithes make the animals subject to tithing rabbinically.

The question being asked here, "Why did they speak of three periods?" seeks

arrival of the [tithing] period it is permitted to sell and slaughter [the animals], but when the period has arrived he must not kill, but if he did, he is exempt.[153]

67. Said Rabbi Jose: it follows that they didn't require the tithing of cattle similar to the time of the formation of fruits[154] nor to [the stage of] one-third [maturity].[155] For if you say "similar to the time of the formation of fruits," it[156] would have taught "all those conceived from the twenty-ninth of Elul."[157] If you say, "according to [the stage of] one-third [maturity]," it would have taught "all those born until the twenty-second of it [Elul]."[158]

68. Rabbi Shammai in the name of Rabbi Abun bar Ḥiyya: they did determine it [tithing of cattle] according to [the stage of] the third [maturity],[159] like Rabbi Simon. For Rabbi Simon said: an animal, though immature,[160] can enter the shed to be tithed.

69. Rabbi Mana rose against Rabbi Shammai. He said to him: you made this statement?[161] Behold we have learned: Ben Azzai says, those born in Elul are tithed by themselves.[162] Is this not even if born until the twenty-ninth of Elul? Must you then say that Ben Azzai is like Rabbi Simon? No. He follows the Rab-

an alternative explanation for the three periods since they didn't serve to separate animals born before and after the tithing period for purposes of the tithe.

153. In Mishnah Bechorot 9:6.

154. The tithing of fruit of a tree follows the blossoming rather than the ripening or harvesting. Before the fifteenth of Shevat, it is tithed for the outgoing year; if after the fifteenth of Shevat, it is tithed for the incoming year. Applying this principle to our case, the conception date of the embryo, not the birth date of the animal, would determine the tithing period.

155. Produce and olives become liable to tithe from the time when they have grown a third. Applying this principle to our case, the animal would have to achieve a certain amount of growth, not a certain measure of time, after birth.

156. Mishnah Bechorot 9:6.

157. Are the new ones.

158. This is, seven days before Rosh Hashanah. We learn from Lev. 22:27: *when a bullock, or a sheep, or a goat, is brought forth, then it shall be seven days under the dam; but from the eighth day on it may be accepted for an offering made by fire unto the Lord.* Hence no animal born after the twenty-second of Elul could be tithed and sacrificed for the old year. Yet our Mishnah includes all those born until the twenty-ninth of Elul.

159. That is, growth of the animal, not conception of the embryo or birth of the animal, determined the time of tithing and subsequent sacrifice.

160. Before the expiration of the seven days after birth.

161. That Rabbi Simon, who said in Mishnah R.H. 1:1 that the New Year for the tithe of animals is the first of Tishri, is the same one who said in Mishnah Bechorot 9:6 that all those born from the first of Tishri to the twenty-ninth of Elul can be combined for the tithe of cattle.

162. Mishnah Bechorot 9:5.

bis.[163] Just as you say according to the Rabbis: leave them and tithe them next year and they will be tithed with those born in the same year, likewise you would say according to Ben Azzai: leave them for the coming period[164] and they will be tithed with those belonging to Elul.

70. Said Rav Huna: it follows that the days in which the first-born is lacking in time [eight days] are included in its year.

71. Said Rabbi Mana: Rabbi Jonah my father learned it from this, *all the firstling males that are born of your herd and of your flock you shall sanctify unto the Lord your God* (Deuteronomy 15:19). How? From the time of its birth you count its year.

Halakhah 2

On the First of Tishri Is the New Year for Years, etc.

1. Whence years?[165] One verse says *and the feast of ingathering, at the end of the year* (Exodus 23:16), and another verse says *and the feast of ingathering, at the turn of*[166] *the year* (Exodus 34:22). Which month contains a festival and an equinox and an ingathering and the [old] year goes out with it[s beginning]? Which one is this? It is Tishri.

2. If you say Tevet, it contains a solstice but it does not contain a festival or an ingathering. If you say Nisan, it contains an equinox and a festival but it does not contain an ingathering. If you say Tammuz, it contains a solstice and an ingathering but it does not contain a festival. And which one is this? It is Tishri.

3. The Fellows [of the Council of Rabbis][167] said before Rabbi Jonah, let it be Tammuz.[168] He said to them, it is written, *in the seventh month* (Leviticus 23:24) and you say thus! They said to him, let it be Tammuz.[169] He said to them, now you are beginning to contend with me concerning the names of the

---

163. Mishnah Bechorot 9:4 reads: all enter the shed to be tithed except *kil'a-yim*, *trefah*, offspring brought forth by means of Caesarean section, an animal too young for sacrifice, and an orphan.

164. The following Passover.

165. What is the basis for our Mishnah which establishes the first of Tishri as the New Year for the reckoning of years?

166. Subsumed under the one Hebrew word *tqufah* are all four turns of the sun, the two equinoxes and the two solstices. To appreciate the word-play in the interpretation which follows, one should substitute *tqufah* for the two translations into "equinox" and the two into "solstice."

167. See footnote 129 above.

168. Implying that the harvest festival of Sukot should be celebrated in Tammuz and that the New Year should begin with Tammuz.

169. Perhaps the seventh month is called Tammuz.

months.[170] For Rabbi Ḥanina said, the names of the months came up with them from Babylonia: originally *in the month Ethanim* (1 Kings 8:2),[171] for in it the patriarchs[172] were born and died, the matriarchs were remembered. Originally *in the month Bul* (1 Kings 6:38),[173] for in it the foliage decays and the earth becomes cloddy; for in it they mix fodder for the cattle from what is stored inside.[174] Originally *in the month Ziv* (1 Kings 6:37), for in it is the bloom of the world. The plants become distinguishable and the trees become distinguishable. Subsequently *and it came to pass in the month Nisan, in the twentieth year* (Nehemiah 2:1); *and it came to pass in the month Kislev, in the twentieth year* (Nehemiah 1:1); *in the tenth month, which is the month Tevet* (Esther 2:16).

4. Rabbi Simon ben Lakesh said, also the names of the angels came up with them from Babylonia: originally *then flew unto me one of the seraphim* (Isaiah 6:6); *above Him stood the seraphim* (Isaiah 6:2). Subsequently *the man Gabriel* (Daniel 9:21); *except Michael your prince* (Daniel 10:21).

5. Concerning Sabbatical years, whence?[175] *At the end of every seven years you shall make a release* (Deuteronomy 15:1). Just as years in general [are counted] from Tishri, so Sabbatical years [are counted] from Tishri.

6. Concerning Jubilee years, whence? *And you shall count seven sabbaths of years, seven times seven years* (Leviticus 25:8). Just as years and Sabbaticals [are counted] from Tishri, so Jubilees [are counted] from Tishri.

7. They raised an objection: but is it not written, *then shall you make proclamation with the blast of the horn [on the tenth day] of the seventh month* (Leviticus 25:9)?[176] Rabbi Jonah and Rabbi Jose, both of them [said] in the name of Rabbi Samuel bar Rav Isaac: so that all months of the year will be equal, no single month be divided between two years.[177]

8. They raised an objection: but behold we learn [in the

170. And the issue is not when the year begins.
171. The whole phrase reads *in the month Ethanim, which is the seventh month.* The word *Ethan* means strong, and hence the comment that in it the patriarchs were born and died.
172. Abraham and Jacob.
173. The whole phrase reads, *in the month Bul, which is the eighth month.*
174. The first etymology of the name *Bul* is based upon its close relationship to the Hebrew words *novel* and *bolot.* The second etymology stresses the relationship to bollim √bll.
175. What is the basis for our Mishnah which establishes the first of Tishri as the New Year for Sabbaticals?
176. Indicating that the Jubilee begins on the tenth of Tishri.

(57a)   Mishnah], on the first of Shevat is the New Year for trees, according to the school of Shammai; the school of Hillel say on the fifteenth. Behold all months of the year are not equal, and a single month is [in fact] divided between two years! [178]

9. How for "young trees"? [179] It is taught: [180] the one who plants, and the one who sinks a vine, and the one who grafts [at least] thirty days before Rosh Hashanah, it is accounted to him as a full year and he is permitted to keep it in the Sabbatical year. Less than thirty days before Rosh Hashanah, it is not accounted to him as a full year, and he is forbidden to keep them in the Sabbatical year.

10. But they said: fruits of this young tree [181] are forbidden until the fifteenth of Shevat. [182]

11. What is the proof? Rabbi Jose in the name of Rabbi Yoḥanan: *and in the fourth year . . .* (Leviticus 19:24). What do you learn from it? Said Rabbi Zeira: *three years it shall be as orlah to you; it shall not be eaten even in the [fourth] year.* [183]

12. Said Rabbi Abba bar Mammal in the presence of Rabbi Zeira: these words appear reasonable when they planted thirty days before Rosh Hashanah, but if they planted less than thirty days before Rosh Hashanah? Come and see, it is accounted to him as a full year and you say thus? [184] He [185] said to him: but if so, [186] even if they planted thirty days before Rosh Hashanah, it

177. If the Jubilee year were to begin on the tenth of Tishri, the preceding days in Tishri would be part of the previous year.

178. If the position of the school of Hillel is followed.

179. See above, footnote 6.

180. In Y. Shevi'it 2:6 and Tosefta 2:3.

181. Using the variant reading *ntiah*, not *ntuyah*.

182. Although for purposes of the Sabbatical year and *Orlah* (Lev. 19:23) we count from Tishri, the school of Hillel places the New Year for trees on the fifteenth of Shevat. Hence we count from the fifteenth of Shevat when determining the proper time to tithe the fruit. With regard to the young tree in question, planted thirty days before Rosh Hashanah (the first of Tishri), its fruit cannot be eaten until the fifteenth of Shevat has passed three times, even though its *Orlah* is completed four and a half months earlier. Hence instead of two years and a month of *Orlah*, there is now an additional four and a half months. Likewise, its fourth year, in which all of its fruit shall be holy for praise-giving unto the Lord (Lev. 19:24), shall be counted from the fifteenth of Shevat to the following fifteenth of Shevat.

183. Rabbi Zeira stresses the vav in *uvashanah*, thus changing the division between verses.

184. That is, would it be necessary to count three full years from Rosh Hashanah and then wait until the fifteenth of Shevat? I have followed the reading in the parallel passage from tractate Shevi'it. Rosh Hashanah, which reads "it is *not* accounted to him as a full year . . . ," does not make sense.

185. Rabbi Zeira.

186. That it is necessary to wait until the fifteenth of Shevat once three full years have passed. *And in the fourth year . . .* (Lev. 19:24) is only expounded to

should be forbidden until thirty days before Rosh Hashanah.[187]

13. What now? Said Rabbi Mana: since it is standing in the year of the tree,[188] it completes its [tree's] year.[189]

14. How for "vegetables"? If a Jew harvested the eve of Rosh Hashanah before nightfall, and a gentile after nightfall, tithe from each of the two separately.[190]

15. Rabbi Zeira, Rabbi Ila, Rabbi Eleazar in the name of Rabbi Hoshaya:[191] one said, most of the rains of the entire year have gone already, and the major part of the cycle[192] has gone. And the other said, until now they [trees] are sustained by the waters of the previous year; henceforth they are sustained by the waters of the coming year. And they didn't know who [of the authorities] said this and who said that.

16. From that which Rabbi Jose said, Rabbi Ila [said] that Rabbi Eleazar [said] in the name of Rabbi Hoshaya: most of the rains of the entire year have gone already, and the major part of the cycle has gone. It must be Rabbi Zeira who said: until now they [trees] are sustained by the waters of the previous year; henceforth they are sustained by the waters of the coming year.

17. A story concerning Rabbi Akiba, who plucked an etrog, and subjected it to the stringencies of the school of Shammai and the stringencies of the school of Hillel.[193] But why specify an etrog? [Why not] even any other tree?[194] It is taught: according to the stringencies of Rabban Gamaliel and according to the

---

indicate a prohibition on the fruit until the fifteenth of Shevat in that case where thirty days are accounted as a year.

187. That is, eliminate the leniency whereby thirty days are accounted as a year and wait three full years.

188. That is, the fifteenth of Shevat.

189. If a tree was planted thirty days before Rosh Hashanah, consider the first thirty days as a year, count two more years from the first of Tishri, and then forbid the fruit additionally until the fifteenth of Shevat.

190. Vegetables gathered after the first of Tishri, the New Year for vegetables, cannot be used as tithe for vegetables gathered before.

191. This is a comment on the Mishnah statement "on the first of Shevat is the New Year for trees." Rabbi Zeira and Rabbi Ila disagree as to what the position of Rabbi Eleazar in the name of Rabbi Hoshaya is.

192. The cycle of Tevet, which begins with the winter solstice.

193. The story is assumed to involve the picking of an etrog on the first of Shevat. Akiba subjected it to two tithes: that of the second year, Second Tithe, following the Hillelite position that the New Year for trees is on the fifteenth of Shevat; and that of the third year, Poorman's Tithe, following the Shammaite position that the New Year for trees is on the first of Shevat.

194. As the incident of Rabbi Akiba is here related, there seems to be no valid reason for specifying an etrog over against any other fruit-bearing tree. Hence it must have been related incorrectly.

stringencies of Rabbi Eleazar.[195] Rabban Gamaliel and Rabbi Eleazar follow the school of Hillel![196]

18. Said Rabbi Jose son of Rabbi Abun: the solution is that it
blossomed before the fifteenth of Shevat of the second [year] and
entered the third [year]. According to the opinion of Rabban
Gamaliel, Poorman's Tithe. According to the opinion of Rabbi
Eleazar, Second Tithe. What did he do? He called its name
[Second] Tithe and redeemed it and gave it to the poor.

Halakhah 3

At Four Times in the Year the World is Judged, etc.

1. Some authorities teach: all of them are judged on Rosh
Hashanah, and the [divine] sentence of each one is sealed on
Rosh Hashanah.
2. Other authorities teach: all of them are judged on Rosh
Hashanah, and the [divine] sentence of each one is sealed on
Yom Kippur.
3. Other authorities teach: all of them are judged on Rosh
Hashanah, and the [divine] sentence of each one is sealed at its
appointed time.
4. Other authorities teach: each one is judged at its appointed
time, and the [divine] sentence of each one is sealed at its appointed time.
5. The Mishnah is like the one who said, all of them are
judged on Rosh Hashanah, and the [divine] sentence of each one
is sealed at its appointed time, for we learn: and on Tabernacles
judgment is passed with respect to water.[197]

195. The reference is to Mishnah Bikkurim 2 : 6. According to Rabban
Gamaliel, the etrog is like a vegetable in that the season of its gathering is the
season for its tithing. Rabbi Eleazar says an etrog is like a tree in all respects.
Hence Rabban Gamaliel determines the tithe-year by when it was plucked,
whereas Eleazar determines the tithe-year by its blossoming. Rabbi Akiba, not
knowing which one to follow, tithed twice.
196. Hence if Rabbi Akiba tithed twice to follow the views of both Rabban
Gamaliel and Rabbi Eleazar, the position of the school of Shammai is irrelevant.
197. Tractate Ta'anit of the Babli, at the beginning of Chapter 1, says: "rain
during the festival is but a sign of divine displeasure." Hence God shows His
pleasure or displeasure at the time of Tabernacles through the giving or withhold-
ing of rain. To gain His blessings for rain, the libation of water was carried out
for seven days at Tabernacles (see Mishnah Sukot 4 : 1) after the morning daily
whole offering. Babli R.H. 16a reads: pour out water before Me on Tabernacles,
so that your rains this year may be blessed.

6. [From] Rav's wording it follows that all of them are judged on Rosh Hashanah and the [divine] sentence of [every] [198] one of them is sealed on Rosh Hashanah.

7. For it teaches in Rav's *Shofar Prayers*: [199] today is the day of the beginning of your works, a memorial to the first day [of Creation]. *For it is a statute for Israel, an ordinance of the God of Jacob.* [200] And on it will be said concerning the nations: which [is destined] for the sword, and which for peace; which for famine, and which for plenty. [201] And on it creatures are passed upon to record them for life or death.

8. But this is not like [the opinion of] Rabbi Jose, for Rabbi Jose [202] said: an individual is judged every moment. What is the proof? *That you should pass judgment upon him every morning, examine him every moment* (Job 7 : 18). *That you should pass judgment upon him every morning*—this refers to his daily sustenance. *Examine him every moment*—this refers to his eating.

9. Rabbi Isaac Rabbah in the name of Rabbi: the king and the public are judged every day. What is the proof? *That He do the judgment of His servant, and the judgment of His people Israel, as every day shall require* (1 Kings 8 : 59). [203]

10. Said Rabbi Levi: *And He will judge the world in righteousness, He will minister judgment to the peoples with equity* (Psalms 9 : 9). [204] The Holy One blessed be He judges Israel by day, at the time when they are occupied with divine command-

198. The genizah fragment reads *shel kol echad v'echad*, although *kol* is not in the Leiden MS.

199. These prayers, supposedly composed by Rav, are found in the Zechronot section of the Rosh Hashanah *Musaf* service.

200. Psalms 81:5. The previous verse, Psalms 81:4, reads: *Blow the horn at the new moon, at the full moon for our feast-day.* Hence the reference is to Rosh Hashanah.

201. A judgment regarding famine or plenty would surely include produce and fruit.

202. The MS reads: "but this is not like R. Yosa, for R. Yosi said." This provides a good example of how loosely equivalent names are used.

203. King Solomon, the speaker, uses the term "His servant" to refer to himself.

204. Rabbi Levi's exposition of the verse takes note of the fact that *tevel* in the A part of the verse parallels *l'umim* in the B part of the verse. Hence if the B part of the verse deals with the judgment of the peoples, the A part must deal with the judgment of Israel.

It is possible that Rabbi Levi derives the lesson that Israel was judged during the daytime, when they were occupied with *mitzvot*, from a play on the word *tevel*. *Tevel* means "world," the literal meaning in Psalms 9:9. Yet it also carries other overtones, as is seen from this comment in Sifre Deut. 37 on Prov. 8:26: "*Tevel*, that is the land of Israel. Why is it called by the name *tevel*? Because of the spice (*tevel*) which is in it. And what is the spice which is in it? The Torah."

ments; and the nations by night, at the time when they have abstained from transgressions.

11. Samuel said: after He judges Israel, He judges the nations.[205]

12. How does Samuel interpret *He will minister judgment to the peoples with equity*? Judge them according to their worthies. He remembers for them the deeds of Jethro, he remembers for them the deeds of Rahab the harlot.[206]

13. Rabbi Hiyya bar Abba asked: produce blasted [by a hot wind] on the eve of Passover, by virtue of which judgment was it smitten?[207] If you say the coming year, it hasn't yet come! If you say the departing year, thus it was waiting the entire year to smite now?[208]

14. Those who die between Rosh Hashanah and Yom Kippur, by virtue of which judgment do they die? If you say the coming year, it hasn't yet come! If you say the departing year, thus they were waiting the entire year to die now?[209]

15. And he did not recall what Rabbi K'rispa in the name of Rabbi Yohanan said, there are three account books [before the Lord]: one for the fully righteous, one for the fully wicked, and one for the intermediates. With regard to that of the fully righteous, they have received verdicts of life by Rosh Hashanah.[210]

Hence *tevel* is identified with the land of Israel and with Torah, the source of all *mitzvot*.

205. This is also a comment upon the verse from Psalms 9:9 in the previous paragraph. The translation is based upon a reading from the genizah MS.

206. In Joshua, chapter 2, Rahab hid the two men sent to spy out Jericho because she believed that the Lord had given over the land to Joshua. As a result, in chapter 6, she and her household were spared to live amidst Israel. And because of his righteousness, Jethro's descendants, the Rechabites, sat with the Sanhedrin in the Temple (b. Sanh. 106a).

207. According to our Mishnah, the world is judged at Passover to ascertain the quality and quantity of produce from then until the subsequent Passover. Hence the question being posed is whether produce smitten on the eve of Passover is smitten by virtue of the previous year's judgment or the impending judgment.

208. It seems hard to accept the claim that a harsh decree upon the produce would be executed only upon the final possible day of the year, with the produce flourishing up to that point.

209. If mortals are judged on Rosh Hashanah, and the final decree for the coming year is sealed on Yom Kippur, then how do we explain those who die between Rosh Hashanah and Yom Kippur? Is it by virtue of the judgment just past on Rosh Hashanah, although the final decree on Yom Kippur has not yet been sealed? Or is it by virtue of the judgment sealed on the previous Yom Kippur? In the latter case he has already lived beyond the period demarcating the past year's deed for consideration.

210. The genizah text has *shelahen* in place of *shelhayyim*. It is interesting to note that someone altered the genizah MS to conform with the reading in the Leiden MS.

With regard to that of the fully wicked, they have received their verdicts by Rosh Hashanah. With regard to that of the intermediates, the ten days of repentance between Rosh Hashanah to Yom Kippur were given to them. If they repented, they are inscribed with the righteous; and if not, they are inscribed with the wicked.

16. What is the proof? *Let them be blotted out of the book*—these are the wicked. *[Of] the living*—these are the righteous. *And not be written with the righteous*—these are the intermediates.[211]

17. Rabbi Ḥananiah, the Fellow of the [Council of] Rabbis, asked: but doesn't the Holy One blessed be He know the future?[212]

18. And he did not recall what Rabbi Simon in the name of Rabbi Joshua ben Levi said: the Holy One blessed be He does not judge man except for the time so far.[213]

19. What is the proof? *Fear not, for God has heard the voice of the lad where he is now* (Genesis 21:17).[214]

20. Rabbi Levi said: *The boasters shall not stand [judgment] in your sight.* Why? Because *You hate all doers of iniquity* (Psalms 5:6).[215]

21. Expounded Rabbi Issachar of K'far Mandi: *For He knows base men; but when He sees iniquity, will he not then consider it?* (Job 11:11).[216]

22. Said Rabbi Joshua ben Levi: *If you were pure and up-*

211. The verse, *Let them be blotted out of the book of the living, and not be written with the righteous*, is from Psalms 69:29.

212. Doesn't He already know on Rosh Hashanah who will repent during the ensuing ten-day period, thus making even judgment of the intermediates possible on Rosh Hashanah? Hence an intermediate could also die between Rosh Hashanah and Yom Kippur.

213. Although God knows all of the man's future acts, yet he is judged only on the acts of the past.

214. "Where he is now," not for the future wickedness of Ishmael.

215. Rabbi Levi is giving an alternative scriptural basis for the view of Rabbi Simon in the name of Rabbi Joshua ben Levi which appears in the text at paragraph 18 above. He notes that, according to the verse, God does not judge those who merely boast to be wicked, only those who do evil. The implication is that although He knows who will do evil in the future, He does not judge them until the evil is actually done.

216. Rabbi Issachar is also giving a scriptural basis for Rabbi Simon's opinion. Job 11:11 is expounded further in Exodus Rabbah III, 2. There the term *mete shav* is explained to mean in context: he knows men who risk death for vanity. Another interpretation given there is: God knows those who are destined to do basely and be killed. The implication here also is that although God may know who is destined to do evil, yet He does not "consider" the iniquity for punishment until He "sees" it take place.

right isn't written here, but *if you are pure and upright* (Job 8:6).[217]

23. Said Rabbi Ḥiyya bar Abba: *The greyhound, the he-goat also, and the king* **alkum** *are with him* (Proverbs 30:31). Customarily, this one seeks for his animal to prevail [in a race], and that one seeks for his animal to prevail. But the Holy One blessed be He is not thus, rather *and the king* **alkum** *is with him*. He does not desire a race against him, because *He will not contend lanetsaḥ [forever]* (Psalms 103:9). He does not contend to prevail.[218]

24. Said Rabbi Eleazar: for the king the law is unwritten.[219]
(57b) Customarily, a king of flesh and blood issues a decree. If he wants, he observes it; if he wants, others observe it.[220] But the Holy One Blessed be He is not thus, rather He issues a decree and observes it first. What is the proof? *They shall keep my precept . . . I am the Lord* (Leviticus 22:9). I am He who kept the precepts of Torah first.

25. Rabbi Simon said: *You shall rise up before the hoary head, and honor the face of the old man, and you shall fear your God: I am the Lord* (Leviticus 19:32). I am He who first fulfilled [the divine commandment of][221] standing before the elder.[222]

26. Rabbi Simon said: *[For what great nation is there that has a god so near to it, as the Lord our God is to us whenever we call upon Him?] And what great nation is there, that has statutes and ordinances so righteous, etc.?* (Deuteronomy 4:7–8).[223]

217. The continuation of the verse reads: *surely now He will awake for you, and make the habitation of your righteousness prosperous.* Hence Rabbi Joshua learns from the verse that, at the moment when one is acting in an upright manner, God will heed him, with no consideration given to what the future might bring.

218. I have left the Hebrew word *alkum* untranslated in the text. In *The Writings*, J.P.S., 1982, the translation is "The king whom none dares resist." In the 1945 J.P.S. Bible translation: "And the king, against whom there is no rising up." The Rabbis understood it otherwise, taking *alkum* to mean "is not contending." The point is that God is objective, not a partisan. The play is upon the words *lanetsaḥ* and *lintsoaḥ*.

219. παρὰ βασιλέως ὁ νόμος ἄγραφος.

220. I am following the readings found in the genizah material: if *he* wants (*rsh*), others observe it. I suspect that the Leiden reading, *rsw*, is in error, since it is seldom the manner of monarchs to allow their subjects freedom of choice with regard to observance of decrees.

221. The genizah MS has: *mitswat 'amidat zaqen*.

222. The reference is probably to the incident of Abraham and the three divine messengers in Gen. 18:22.

223. The genizah MS cites Deut. 4:7. The Leiden MS seems to have combined verses 7 and 8.

27. Rabbi Ḥama the son of Rabbi Ḥanina and Rabbi Hoshaya: one said, is there a nation like this nation! Customarily, a man who knows that he is on trial wears black, and wraps himself in black, and lets his beard grow, for he doesn't know how his trial will turn out. But Israel is not thus, rather they wear white, and wrap themselves in white, and shave their beards, and eat, drink, and rejoice. They know that the Holy One Blessed be He does for them miracles.

28. And the other [authority] said, is there a nation like this nation! Customarily, the ruler says the trial is today, and the robber says tomorrow is the trial. To whom do they listen? Is it not to the ruler? But the Holy One Blessed be He is not thus. The Bet Din said: today is Rosh Hashanah. The Holy One Blessed be He says to the ministering angels: set up the platform, let the defenders rise and let the prosecutors rise; for my children have said, today is Rosh Hashanah. If the Bet Din changed to make the month full [so that Rosh Hashanah will fall on the morrow], the Holy One Blessed be He says to the ministering angels: remove the platform,[224] remove the defenders, and remove the prosecutors; for my children have decided to make the month full [making Rosh Hashanah fall on the morrow]. What is the proof? *For it is a statute for Israel, an ordinance of the God of Jacob* (Psalms 81:5).[225] If it is not *a statute for Israel*, as though it were possible, it is not *an ordinance of the God of Jacob.*[226]

29. Rabbi K'rispa in the name of Rabbi Yoḥanan: in the past *these are the appointed seasons of the Lord*; subsequently *which you shall proclaim* (Leviticus 23:4).

30. Said Rabbi Ila: if you designate them [with the biblical phrase] *My appointed seasons* (Leviticus 23:2), they are My appointed seasons, and if not, they are not My appointed seasons.

31. Rabbi Simon said: *many things have You done, O Lord my God, even Your wondrous works, and Your thoughts toward us* (Psalms 40:6). In the past *many things have you done.* Subsequently *Your works and Your thoughts toward us.*

32. Said Rabbi Levi: [this can be compared] to a king who had a time-piece. When his son grew up, he handed it over to him.[227]

224. The next word in the Hebrew text, *lmaḥar*, is erased in the Leiden MS and absent in the genizah MS. I have eliminated it in my translation.
225. The previous verse reads: *blow the horn at the new moon, at the full moon for our feast-day.* Hence the reference is to Rosh Hashanah.
226. That is, the festival derives its divine character by virtue of Israel's observance of it.
227. The analogy is to God, Israel, and the ability to set festivals.

33. Said Rabbi Jose bar Ḥanina: [this can be compared] to a king who had a bracelet.[228] When his son grew up, he handed it over to him.

34. Said Rabbi Aḥa: [this can be compared] to a king who had a [signet] ring. When his son grew up, he handed it over to him.

35. Said Rabbi Ḥiyya bar Abba: [this can be compared] to an artisan who had carpenter's tools. When his son grew up, he handed them[229] over to him.

36. Said Rabbi Isaac: [this can be compared] to a king who had storehouses. When his son grew up, he handed them over to him.

37. And the Rabbis said: [this can be compared] to a physician who had a medicine chest. When his son grew up, he handed it over to him.

38. And on Rosh Hashanah all mortals[230] pass before him *kivno maron.*[231] Rabbi Aḥa said: like those [from] sheds.[232] And

---

228. This translation was suggested by Stephen Kaufman because of context. In his book *The Akkadian Influences on Aramaic* (University of Chicago Press, 1974), p. 102, he cites Perles in *Orientalistische Literaturzeitung* 21:70, who suggests that the Akkadian word *šemiru* is the origin of the rare rabbinic Hebrew word *šûmêrāh*. Perles cites Pesikta Kahana Buber 53b, but the term does not appear there. Kaufman rejects Perles' suggestion on phonetic grounds, but agrees that the Akkadian *sêmiru* might well be the source of the word intended here and that *šûmêrāh* is the result of a textual corruption. He speculates that the intended Hebrew word was probably some form of *šêr* (see Jastrow, p. 1568). Jastrow, p. 1537, translates as "watch-tower."

229. Following the reading *msrn* from the genizah MS.

230. Literally, those who come into the world.

231. In the Leiden MS, *kvno maron*; in the genizah MS, *kvnwmrwn*; in the Tosefta, *nwmrwn*. Babli R.H. 18a has *kvnei maron*; the Babli text then goes on to give three possible interpretations. The first is "like a flock of sheep," the interpretation being based upon a connection between *maron* and the Aramaic *'imrana*, lamb. The image presented, if this interpretation is followed, is that of a flock of sheep passing through a narrow gateway so that they can be counted one by one. Resh Lakish suggests the interpretation: "As in the ascent of Bet Maron." However, many versions read *kma'alot bet ḥoron*. Lieberman, in *Tosefta Kifshutah*, Part V, p. 1022, n. 9, suggests that *ḥoron* was changed to *maron* to provide a play on the term being expounded, *kvnei maron*. Rav Judah in the name of Samuel suggests: "like the armies of the house of David." Here the interpretation is based upon a combining of *kvno maron* (the reading we have in the Leiden MS) into *kvnumron* (the genizah MS reading), which means "as in a division of troops." Lieberman concludes that without a doubt the correct interpretation is "as in a division of troops."

232. The reference probably being to flocks coming out of the shed one by one to be tithed. The interpretation of Rabbi Aḥa, understood this way, would favor the Babli interpretation of *bnei maron* as "like a flock of sheep." Lieberman, *Tosefta Kifshutah*, suggests that the intended word is the Greek δειράδιν, δειράδιον. Hence Rabbi Aḥa's interpretation would be: "like those [from] a narrow mountain ridge." Lieberman sees in Rabbi Aḥa's interpretation the image of a division on a narrow path on a mountain summit. Therefore it would resemble

the Rabbis said: like *Benumin*.[233]

39. What is the proof? *He that fashions the hearts of them all, that considers all their doings* (Psalms 33:15). Said Rabbi Levi: He that fashions the hearts of them all had considered all their doings.[234]

40. Said Rabbi Eleazar: customarily, which is easier for the potter? To make one hundred vessels or to look at them? Is it not to look at them?[235]

41. Said Rabbi Berakia: their Creator desires that their hearts be solely [directed] to Him.[236]

42. Said Rabbi Abun: He who is unique in His world has considered all their doings.[237]

43. And on Tabernacles judgment is passed with respect to water.[238] This Mishnah is by Rabbi Akiba, for Rabbi Akiba said: the water libation is a Torah precept. On the second [day of Tabernacles], *and their drink offerings* (Numbers 29:19). On the sixth [day of Tabernacles], *and his drink offering* (Numbers 29:31). On the seventh [day of Tabernacles], *after the ordinance* (Numbers 29:33). *Mem yod mem—mayim* [water].[239]

44. Scripture says: bring the first barley at Passover that the produce may be blessed for you. Bring the first wheat at the Festival of Weeks that the fruits of the tree may be blessed for you. It follows:[240] the water libation on Tabernacles, that the waters may be blessed for you.

45. Taught Rabbi Simon ben Yoḥai: behold if Israel was worthy

---

Resh Lakish's interpretation in the Babli—*kma'alot bet ḥoron*—soldiers going up the ascent one by one.

233. Lieberman, *Tosefta Kifshutah*, p. 1023, suggests that the genizah reading *beinumin* is a compound of *bet numin*, the name of a place now unknown to us.

234. This is the way Rabbi Levi understands the verse.

235. The potter makes one vessel at a time and can only look at them all after he has finished, since while he is working he must concentrate solely on the one before him. According to the verse from Psalms 33, God is not so. At the time when He is creating, He is also understanding completely all of His Creations.

236. This is the way Rabbi Berakia understands Psalms 33:15. He expounds *yaḥad* as *yaḥid*.

237. Rabbi Abun expounds *hayoṣer yaḥad* as *hayoṣer yaḥid*.

238. See above, Halakhah 3, paragraph 5.

239. The derivation of *mayim* from the Torah is based upon a careful reading of the text. In Scriptures a formula which enumerates the offerings is repeated for each day of Tabernacles. However, three variations can be found. On days 1, 3, 4, and 7, the word *wniska* is used. On day 2, *wniskéhem*; the *mem* is extraneous. On day 6, *unsakheha*; the *yod* is extraneous. On days 2 through 6, the word *kmishpat* is used. On day 7, *kmishpatam*; the *mem* is extraneous. The assumption is that these extraneous letters were introduced advisedly to spell out *mayim*.

240. That is, conclude from the above.

on Rosh Hashanah and plentiful rain was decreed for them, but in the end they sinned, to diminish them [the rains] is impossible, since the decree was already issued. What does the Holy One Blessed be He do? He scatters them [the rains] to the seas, deserts, and rivers so that the land will not benefit from them. What is the proof? *To cause it to rain on a land where no man is, on the wilderness in which there is no man* (Job 38 : 26).

46. Behold if Israel was not worthy on Rosh Hashanah and limited rain was decreed for them, but in the end they repented, to augment them [the rains] is impossible, since the decree was already issued. What does the Holy One Blessed be He do for them? He brings down as much as is required for the land and causes with them dew and winds in order that the land will benefit from them. What is the proof? *Watering her ridges abundantly, settling down the furrows thereof, you make her soft with showers, you bless the growth thereof* (Psalms 65 : 11).

47. *Drought and heat consume the snow waters; so does the nether world those that have sinned* (Job 24 : 19). Because of transgressions done by Israel in the summer, they were deprived of the snow waters.

48. It is written: *the eyes of the Lord your God are always upon it [the land of Israel], from the beginning of the year* (Deuteronomy 11 : 12). Kahana said: *from the poverty of* is written.[241] *And to the end of the year.* He afflicts it in its beginning, and He gives it a good end at the close.

Halakhah 4

Because of Six New Moons the Messengers Go Forth, etc.

1. And let them go out also because of the Festival of Weeks? The Festival of Weeks had been fixed.[242] Hence, you are saying sometimes [the Festival of Weeks falls on] the fifth [of Sivan], sometimes the sixth, sometimes the seventh.[243] When the months

241. In Scriptures, the word is written defectively without the aleph, *mereshit*, which can be derived from the root *rsh*, poor. Hence Kahana seems to be stressing the poorness of spirit with which Israel comes before God on Rosh Hashanah and Yom Kippur—with prayer, petition, and fasting—and the abundant harvests which result from proper repentance.
242. It is the fiftieth day from the second day of Passover. Since our Mishnah says that messengers go out to inform concerning the new moon of Nisan, a messenger for Shavuot is unnecessary.
243. In the month of Sivan.

are full, the fifth; in their order, the sixth; defective, the seventh.[244]

2. But did they not go out in Elul?[245] Only to declare that the moon was sanctified [did messengers go out in Tishri].[246]

3. Said Rabbi Joshua ben Levi: I vouch to those [messengers] who go to Nimrin that not one of them will die while going.[247]

4. There they are troubled for the great fast [of Yom Kippur] two days.[248] Rav Ḥisda said to them: why do you enter to such straits? The presumption is that the Bet Din is not remiss with regard to it.[249]

5. The father of Rabbi Samuel bar Rav Isaac was troubled and fasted two days. His intestines ceased functioning and he died.

Halakhah 5

Whether [the New Moon] Was Seen Clearly or Whether It Was Not Seen Clearly, etc.

1. What is the meaning of *b'alil*? Exposed, as you find it said: *as purified silver exposed to the earth, refined seven times* (Psalms 12:7).[250]

Halakhah 6

1. Here is a story: more than forty pairs [of witnesses] were passing [through] and Rabbi Akiba detained them in Lod be-

244. "Full" means if both Nisan and Iyar have thirty days. "In their natural order" means one is full and one defective. "Defective" means both have twenty-nine days.

245. According to our Mishnah, they went out in Elul to inform the diaspora of the day on which *Rosh Ḥodesh* Elul fell. From this day alone, the people could ascertain the day of Rosh Hashanah, Yom Kippur, and Sukot without need for messengers in Tishri.

246. Although one might assume that Rosh Hashanah would be thirty days after *Rosh Ḥodesh* Elul, yet during any given year the possibility was present that the Bet Din might make Elul full.

247. Nimrin, a place in Syria, is the last station of messengers proclaiming the New Moon. Rabbi Joshua's guarantee applies for the duration of the trip to Nimrin and back.

248. They are troubled because they don't know if Elul was full and hence they observe two days.

249. And therefore if no messenger arrives to tell you that Elul was made full, it is safe to assume that Elul is twenty-nine days and you have no reason for doubt concerning the correct day of Yom Kippur.

250. The J.P.S. translation is: *as silver tried in a crucible on the earth*. Here,

cause there were as many as forty pairs. But if there were but one pair, he wouldn't have detained them.

2. Rabban Gamaliel sent to him [an admonishment]: if you detain the many, the result will be that you will cause them to stumble in the time to come.[251] [Will not your action] result in preventing many from performing a religious precept? And anyone who detains the multitude from doing a religious precept requires excommunication.

3. Said Rabbi Judah the baker: heaven forfend Rabbi Akiba was not put under ban! It was Zekher the head of Gir [or Geder], and Gamaliel sent and removed him from his office.

Halakhah 7

If a Father and a Son Saw the New Moon, etc.

1. The proof of Rabbi Simon[252] [is] like it was at the beginning: *and God said to Moses and to Aaron, this New Moon is to you the beginning of months etc.* (Exodus 12 : 1).[253]

Halakhah 8[254]

Said Rabbi Jose: Once Tobiah the Physician Saw the New Moon, etc.

1. The priests accepted him and his son but disqualified his slave as unfit [for testimony]. But when they came before the Court, they accepted him and his slave and disqualified his son as a relative.[255]

---

however, the verse is used to mean above the earth, in a location clearly visible.

251. They will assume that they were not needed, as others will have seen the moon. Hence few if any would be willing to make the necessary effort to take the trip in the future, if they thought that unless they were first to arrive there was no purpose for them to do so. R. Akiba detained them to prevent an unnecessary Sabbath desecration.

252. That a father and son and all relatives are eligible to testify to the appearance of the New Moon.

253. Yet Moses and Aaron were brothers.

254. On Mishnah 9.

255. Near relatives are not permitted to testify together.

Halakhah 9[256]

(57c)   1. These are disqualified: one who plays with *quviya*. [That is,] the one who plays with dice,[257] whether one plays with dice or plays with shells of nuts and pomegranates.

2. When can they[258] reaccept him? After he breaks his dice and is examined and [it is found that] he has repented completely.

3. A lender on interest: one who lends on interest. From what time can they[258] reaccept them? After he tears up his documents and is examined and [it is found that] he has repented completely.

4. Pigeon-flyers: [that is,] one who races pigeons [and wagers on them]. [This applies] whether one races pigeons or races any other domestic animal, beast of chase, or bird. From what time can they[258] reaccept him? After he breaks his *pegmas*[259] and is examined and [it is found that] he has repented completely.

5. A trader in produce of the Sabbatical year: [that is,] one who is a specialist in the trade of the Sabbatical year. Who is a specialist in the trade of the Sabbatical year?[260] He who sits idly the entire cycle. When the Sabbatical year arrived, he begins to put forth his hands and deal in fruits of sin. From what time can they[258] reaccept him? After the next Sabbatical year arrives and he is examined and [it is found that] he has repented completely.

6. It was taught: Rabbi Jose says two Sabbaticals.

7. It was taught in the name of Rabbi Nehemiah: monetary restitution, not words. And he should say: [I give] to you 200 zuz; distribute among the poor, from what I profited of fruits of sin.

8. They added to them[261] the shepherds and extortionists and robbers and all those who are suspected of appropriating goods of others; their testimony is invalid.

9. Said Rabbi Abbahu: only when they are tending small cattle.[262]

---

256. On Mishnah 10.
257. The Greek loan-word *quviya* has been defined with the word *psifsin*, which also means cubes or dice.
258. The Bet Din.
259. A contrivance for the bird-catcher made of boards (Krauss); a kind of trap or snare or a dovecote (*The Aruch*, Levy).
260. I have followed the reading from the parallels: *ei zehu teger shvi'it*.
261. To those enumerated in the Mishnah.
262. I am following the variant reading *bhemah daqah*. There is a difference between cows and such animals as sheep and goats because the smaller animals more easily escape into fields belonging to others.

10. Said Rav Huna: who is the authority for "those who let pigeons fly"? Rabbi Eleazar.

11. For we learn there [in a Mishnah] [263] two [teachings] in the name of Rabbi Eleazar: a woman may go out [on the Sabbath] wearing a "city of gold," [264] and those who let pigeons fly are disqualified from testimony.

12. Said Rabbi Mana in the presence of Rabbi Jose: is all that in Tractate Sanhedrin [Mishnah 3 : 3] like Rabbi Eleazar? [265] He [266] said to him: it is a unanimous opinion. How is it a unanimous opinion? [267] Thus said Rabbi Jose: we know that he [268] is disqualified from testimony in monetary matters. [269] What does it [the Mishnah in Eduyot] come to tell? [270] Just as he is disqualified from testimony in monetary matters, likewise he is disqualified from testimony in capital cases.

13. And witnesses regarding the [new] month are like witnesses regarding capital cases? [271] But behold it teaches [in the Mishnah]: it is a general rule that for any testimony for which a woman is disqualified these also are disqualified. [272]

14. Who taught it? The Rabbis? Could the Rabbis agree with Rabbi Eleazar and [at the same time] differ with him? [273]

263. Mishnah Eduyot 2 : 7.

264. A kind of hat.

265. That is, since from Mishnah Eduyot we learn that Rabbi Eleazar was the authority who declared those who let pigeons fly to be disqualified from testimony, does it follow that the other categories as well as pigeon-flyers disqualified rabbinically in Mishnah Sanhedrin 3 : 3 are in accordance with the opinion of Rabbi Eleazar?

266. Rabbi Jose.

267. How is it possible to maintain that Sanhedrin 3 : 3 is a unanimous opinion, whereas Eduyot 2 : 7 is the view of Rabbi Eleazar?

268. The pigeon-flyer.

269. From the Mishnah in Sanhedrin.

270. Literally "testify," a play on *Eduyot*. What additional information do we get from the teaching of Rabbi Eleazar in Eduyot?

271. If we say that the authority for "those who let pigeons fly" here in Mishnah Rosh Hashanah is Rabbi Eleazar, we are saying that testimony regarding the moon is like testimony in capital cases! Yet we know that testimony regarding the moon is like testimony regarding monetary matters; Mishnah Rosh Hashanah is like Mishnah Sanhedrin 3 : 3; the authority for "those who let pigeons fly" is a unanimous rabbinic opinion.

272. If the Mishnah follows the opinion of Rabbi Eleazar, the statement is clear, since women are acceptable for testimony only in the case of the *agunah*, and those disqualified by the Mishnah are unacceptable in all cases. If the Mishnah follows the opinion of the Rabbis, those specified in the Mishnah are disqualified only in cases of monetary matters, whereas women are disqualified in all cases. Hence the general rule would seem to support the contention that the Mishnah follows Rabbi Eleazar.

273. For the Rabbis, the Mishnah would have to deal only with financial cases.

15. Rabbi Jonah in the name of Rav Huna: all of them are of Rabbi Eleazar. The differences in this case are based on the same principles as the differences in the following case.

16. For it is taught: a false witness is disqualified for all testimony in the Torah; the opinion of Rabbi Meir. Said Rabbi Jose: when? Only if he is found perjured in a capital case. But if he is found perjured in a case involving money, in monetary cases [alone] he is suspect and hence disqualified [from it only].

17. The opinion of Rabbi Jose is like the Rabbis, and that of Rabbi Meir is like Rabbi Eleazar.

Halakhah 10

1. Said Rabbi Isaac: the Torah[274] speaks in all kinds of imprecise idioms: *and the man wondered at her* (Genesis 24:21),[275] "any jar holding two seahs" (Mishnah Terumot 10:8),[276] "if one is waiting in ambush for them, they may carry staves."[277]

2. One might think that just as they may profane the Sabbath to testify concerning them,[278] likewise they may profane the Sabbath to announce that they [the dates of the New Moon] have been set?[279] Scripture teaches *which you shall proclaim* (Leviticus 23:4). Concerning their proclamation [only], you may profane the Sabbath; you may not profane the Sabbath to announce that they have been set.

3. Rabbi Simon ben Lakish asked: the cutting of the *Omer*,[280] does it override the Sabbath during the day?[281]

274. That is, Scriptures as well as the Rabbis.
275. Korban Ha'edah points out that the verb *mishta'e* from this scriptural verse implies also the meaning which would be explicit were the verse to read *vha'ish mishtomem aleha*. Hence he was desolated by her as he stood wondering and astonished.
276. The implication from Mishnah Terumot 10:8 is not only that the jar should have a capacity of two seahs, but that in actuality it should contain two seahs.
277. The imprecision in language here in our Mishnah is that an ambush is by definition a surprise attack. Hence how would they know to carry staves on the Sabbath to defend themselves?
278. The appearance of New Moons.
279. That is, just as witnesses may profane the Sabbath so as to arrive in time to testify, likewise you might think that the messengers to the diaspora might profane the Sabbath to speed their trips.
280. The *Omer* is the first sheaf cut during the barley harvest, which was offered in the Temple as a sacrifice on the second day of Passover. Before the offering of this sacrifice, it was forbidden to eat the new grain.
281. When the sixteenth of Nisan falls on Sabbath. The *Omer* is to be reaped

4. Answered Rabbi Abbayi: behold we have learned that its precept is to reap by night; yet if reaped by day, it is valid and it overrides the Sabbath. But he didn't accept it.[282]

5. Rabbi Aḥa said that Rabbi Simon ben Lakish retracted [his objection] because of this:[283] when it became dark he said to them, "has the sun set?" They say, "yes." "Has the sun set?" They say, "yes."[284] What are we discussing?[285] If [reaping on Sabbath by] night, he [the author of the Mishnah] already said.[286] But if it is not a matter of night, interpret it as a matter of [reaping on the Sabbath by] day.

6. Anything that supersedes the Sabbath during the day, do its preparatory acts supersede the Sabbath the previous night?[287] But behold we have learned,[288] they placed the makers of the cakes to prepare their cake.[289] It may be interpreted rather as [dealing solely with] a weekday.

7. Taught Rabbi Ḥiyya bar Ada: this is the order of the *Tamid* for the service of the House of our God, whether on a weekday or the Sabbath.

8. But behold, we have learned:[290] they reaped it, put it into

---

by night. Hence if the first day of the festival falls on Friday, the reaping of the *Omer* is carried out on Friday night, and this overrides the Sabbath. The question here is whether it is also valid to reap the *Omer* during the day, and whether such reaping would override the Sabbath. The issue is complicated by Mishnah 2 : 6 in Megillah. This is the general principle: any commandment which is to be performed by day may be performed during the whole of the day, and any commandment which is to be performed by night may be performed during the whole of the night. In b. Menachot 72a, Rabbi Eleazar the son of Rabbi Simon says: the *Omer* that was reaped not in accordance with its prescribed rite is invalid.

282. Rabbi Simon ben Lakish understood "and it overrides the Sabbath" to refer to reaping on the night of the sixteenth.

283. Mishnah Menachot 10 : 3.

284. The Mishnah continues: on the Sabbath he called out further, "on this Sabbath?" And they answered, "yes." "On this Sabbath?" And they answered, "yes." "Shall I reap?" And they answered, "reap." "Shall I reap?" And they answered, "reap."

285. In the phrase "and it overrides the Sabbath" from Mishnah Menachot 10 : 3.

286. In Mishnah Menachot 10 : 3.

287. The question deals with preparatory acts which cannot be done before the Sabbath begins.

288. In Mishnah Tamid 1 : 3.

289. This cake was being prepared for the morning offering, and since it was still prior to daybreak, it would seem that such preparatory acts superseded the Sabbath at night.

290. Mishnah Menachot 10 : 4. This refers to the night of the sixteenth of Nisan.

the baskets, brought it to the Temple Court, and they used to parch it with fire in order to fulfill thereby the precept of parched ears;[291] the opinion of Rabbi Meir. Said Rabbi Jose: inasmuch as he commenced the commandment [of parching], they say to him, finish it![292]

9. Retorted Rabbi Judah the Cappadocian in the presence of Rabbi Jose: suppose[293] it came from the attic.[294] Inasmuch as he did not commence the commandment [of parching], they don't say to him, finish it.[295]

10. Challenged Rabbi Jacob bar Susi: but behold, we have learned that for as much as a night and a day's journey they were allowed to profane the Sabbath and go to testify concerning the New Moon.[296] He [Rabbi Jose] said to them: since the day requires night, and the night requires day,[297] it is as if it were entirely day.[298]

11. Said Rabbi Jose the son of Rabbi Abun: and is it not sanctified retroactively?[299] Since it is sanctified retroactively, day and night are one.[300]

291. Lev. 2:14. Hence the activities mentioned above are acts carried out during the previous night preparatory to the meal-offering of the *Omer*.

292. Since the initial preparatory act, the reaping, supersedes the Sabbath, the remainder of the required preparatory acts are allowed to follow.

293. Literally, put yourself in the position.

294. Where the old produce is stored. That is, suppose the *Omer* came from the choicest of the old produce since, when it falls on the Sabbath, they use old produce. Then they do not parch the ears, since reaping had not preceded.

295. Following the variant reading *shelo hithil* from Megillah, chap. 2, Hal. 7.

296. The profaning of the Sabbath by night was thus an act preparatory to the sanctification by day.

297. After seeing the moon, it may be necessary to begin the trip at night so as to arrive in time during the day.

298. The distinction between profaning during the night or during the day is meaningless here.

299. That is, the Bet Din waited the entire thirtieth day, and no witnesses arrived. Therefore they intercalated the month. If on a later day witnesses arrived to say that they saw the moon in its proper time, and if the validity of their testimony can be established, the formerly intercalated day is removed. Why, then, profane the Sabbath night at all?

300. The argument of retroactivity serves to show that it is, strictly speaking, unnecessary to profane at all. However, if the goal is to testify so that the moon will be sanctified at the appropriate time, the entire Sabbath, night as well as day, should be treated as a unit. P'ne Moshe has a different interpretation.

2 Mishnah Rosh Hashanah Chapter Two

1. If they[1] do not know him[2], they[3] send another[4] with him to testify of him.[5] Originally they used to accept testimony about the New Moon from any man;[6] after the *minim* ruined that system,[7] they[8] enacted that it would only be accepted from persons known.[9] Formerly they used to light beacons;[10] after the Samaritans ruined that system,[11] they enacted that messengers should go forth.

2. How did they light the beacons? They used to bring long poles of cedar-wood and reeds and olive-wood and hatcheled flax

1. The Bet Din in Jerusalem.
2. That is, if it is a priori evident to the local authorities that the Bet Din in Jerusalem cannot be confident of the trustworthiness of the witness.
3. The authorities of his local community.
4. A witness acknowledged as trustworthy. The Tosefta parallel reads "they send his witnesses," but variants also give the reading "his witness." The Babylonian Talmud interprets "another" in the plural sense of "another pair of witnesses," whereas the Palestinian Talmud takes "another" in the singular sense.
5. To vouch for his credibility.
6. That is, from any Jewish male who fulfills the requisite qualifications.
7. By hiring and sending false witnesses. The *minim* mentioned here are probably Sadducees, who attempted to manipulate the calendar according to their belief that Passover should fall on the Sabbath and the second day on a Sunday. That way the first day of the *Omer* would be literally "on the morrow of the Sabbath," which is how they understood Lev. 23:11. See Chagigah, chapter 2, Mishnah 4, for the debate between Bet Hillel and Bet Shammai on the proper day of the Festival of Weeks.
8. The Bet Din.
9. To the Bet Din and acknowledged as trustworthy, or else accompanied by emissaries who would vouch for their credibility.
10. To notify the diaspora in Babylonia of the New Moon, they lit beacons on the night which begins the thirty-first day if the thirtieth day had been declared *Rosh Ḥodesh*.
11. By lighting beacons on the night which begins the thirty-first day in full months, thus causing the Babylonians to think the month was defective.

and one would bind them[12] together with cord. And someone
would go up to the top of the hill and set fire to them and wave
them to and fro, up and down, until he saw his fellow [signaller]
doing likewise on the top of the second hill. And likewise on the
top of the third hill.

3. From where did they used to light beacons? From the
Mount of Olives [they signalled] to Sartaba, and from Sartaba to
Agrippina, and from Agrippina to Hauran, and from Hauran to
Bet Baltin. And beyond Bet Baltin they did not budge, but some-
one waved it[13] to and fro, up and down, until he could see the
entire diaspora before him like a blazing fire.

4. A large courtyard called Bet Ya'azek was in Jerusalem, and
there all the witnesses gathered, and there the Bet Din examined
them. And they used to prepare for them abundant feasts, so
that they would become accustomed to coming.[14]

5. Formerly they would not budge from there all the day;[15]
then Rabban Gamaliel the Elder decreed that they might walk
two thousand cubits in any direction. And not only these [were
permitted this leniency], but also the midwife who comes to aid
in childbirth, and the one who comes to save from a fire, from
an invading troop, from a flooding river, from a fallen building;
behold these are considered as natives of the town and they are
permitted two thousand cubits in any direction.

6. How do they examine the witnesses? They first examine
the pair that arrived first. They bring in the elder of the two and
(57d)   say to him: "tell us how you saw the moon. In front of the sun,
or behind the sun? To the north of it or to the south of it? What
was its height and in which direction was it inclined? And what
was its width?" If he said "in front of the sun," he has not said
anything.[16]

7. They used to bring in the second and examine him. If
their words[17] were found to coincide, their testimony was estab-

12. Following a variant reading.
13. The kindled beacon.
14. Such feasts would serve, at least in part, as additional motivation to make
the trip.
15. On the Sabbath after they had testified.
16. Immediately before the *molad*, the moon is west of the sun near the horizon, and it descends before sunset, hence appearing to be "in front of the sun."
After the *molad*, it is seen east of the sun above the horizon and it is visible after
sunset. Hence its description as "behind the sun." There are those who explain
"in front of the sun" as with the horns of the crescent facing the sun. If the
witness claimed to have seen it "in front of the sun," he saw either the old moon
or something other than the moon.
17. The accounts of both witnesses.

lished. With regard to the remaining pairs, they questioned them concerning the main points, not because they needed them, but in order that they would not leave in disappointment so that they would become accustomed to coming.

8. The head of the Bet Din says: "It is sanctified!" And all of the people answer after him: "It is sanctified! It is sanctified!" They proclaim it sanctified whether or not it is seen in its proper time. Rabbi Eleazar son of Rabbi Zadok says: if it is not seen in its proper time, they do not proclaim it sanctified, because heaven has already sanctified it.

9. Rabban Gamaliel had a diagram of phases of the moon on a tablet and on the wall in his upper chamber, so that with them he would show the ordinary people and say: did you see it like this or like this? Once two came and said: we saw it in the morning in the east and in the evening in the west. Rabbi Yoḥanan said: they are false witnesses! But when they came to Yavneh, Rabban Gamaliel accepted them.

10. And two others came and said: we saw it in its proper time, but it did not appear on [the night of] its intercalation;[18] yet Rabban Gamaliel accepted them. Said Rabbi Dosa ben Harkinus: they are false witnesses! How can people testify regarding a woman that she gave birth, when behold her belly is between her teeth? Rabbi Joshua said to him: I understand your point.

11. Rabban Gamaliel sent to him:[19] I order you to come to me with your staff and your money on the day that works out to be the Day of Atonement according to your calculation. Rabbi Akiba went and found him[19] distressed. He said to him:[19] I can show that whatever Rabban Gamaliel has done is legitimate, because the verse says: *these are the appointed seasons of the Lord, even holy convocations which you shall proclaim* (Leviticus 23:4). Whether in their proper time or not, I have no "appointed seasons" except for these.

12. He[19] went to Rabbi Dosa ben Harkinus, who said to him: if we wish to argue concerning [decisions of] the Bet Din of Rabban Gamaliel, we must argue concerning [decisions of] every Bet Din that has arisen from the days of Moses until now, because the verse says: *Then went up Moses, and Aaron, Nadab, and Abihu, and seventy of the elders of Israel* (Exodus 24:9). And why were the names of the elders not specified. In order to

---

18. It was seen on the night of the thirtieth, so the month was declared defective. Yet it was not seen after nightfall on the thirty-first, i.e. the second, when, assuming clear weather, it should have been even more visible.

19. R. Joshua ben Ḥananiah.

teach you that every threesome that was constituted as a Bet Din
over Israel, behold they are like the Bet Din of Moses. He took
his staff and his money in his hand, and he went to Rabban
Gamaliel at Yavneh on the day that worked out to be the Day of
Atonement according to his calculation. Rabban Gamaliel arose
and kissed him on his head and said to him: come in peace, my
teacher and my disciple. My teacher in wisdom, and my disciple
because you accepted my words.

Halakhah 1

An Unknown Witness

Gemara. 1. If they do not know him, etc. Rabbi Jonah said,
it should have been necessary to teach thus: originally they used
to accept testimony about the New Moon from any man. If they
didn't know him, they used to send another with him to testify
of him.[20]

2. Said Rabbi Jose, even in accordance with [the order of]
our Mishnah it is acceptable: If they do not know him, they send
another with him to testify of him. Why?[21] Because originally
[before the evil acts of the *minim*] they used to accept testimony
about the New Moon from any man, etc.

3. And is the statement of one witness sufficient?[22] From
your own, it is given to you: since legally witnesses are not necessary,[23] and they said that witnesses are necessary,[24] they said
that the statement of one witness is sufficient.

4. Can one witness be relied upon like two? How can this
be?[25] If there was one who knows his own handwriting and the
handwriting of his fellow, and one whom no one except his fel-

20. R. Jonah reverses the order of the first two sentences in the Mishnah. If
the Bet Din in Jerusalem would not know a witness, and hence be confident of
his reliability, the local court would send another from his own town with him in
order to attest to his eligibility and trustworthiness as a witness. In this way, they
could allay any fears that he might be a *min* or a hireling of *minim*.

21. Every male Jew is assumed to be a *kosher* witness; hence why the attesting
witness?

22. Is it possible that sending along only one witness from his town to accompany him and to attest to his credentials before the *Bet Din Hagadol* is sufficient? According to Deut. 19:15, "a case can be valid only on the testimony of
two witnesses or more."

23. Every male Jew is presumed a *kosher* and reliable witness unless evidence
to the contrary is produced. Hence witnesses to attest to the witness would be
unnecessary.

24. The Rabbis said that witnesses are necessary in order to protect against
deceit from the *minim*.

25. That is, name a case to which this rule will apply.

low knows, is his fellow combined with one from the street to testify of him?[26]

5. Rabbi Zeira [in the name of] Rav Huna in the name of Rav: he and another are not combined [to testify] concerning the signature of the second witness.[27]

We need to inquire about this case: there were two [witnesses]: One—everyone knows his handwriting, and one—no one except his fellow knows it [his handwriting].[28] Is his fellow made like one from the street to testify of him?[29]

If so,[30] the result would be that the entire testimony[31] is established by one witness!

6. Rabbi Judah said: and it is right. Behold, if two went out from a certain city where the majority are non-Jews, like this Susita; one—everyone knows that he is a Jew, and the other—no one knows him but his fellow, should his fellow[32] be made like one from the street to testify of him?[33] If you say yes, is not the result that the entire testimony is established by one witness?[34]

26. The case cited follows the reading in P.T. Ketubot 2, Hal. 4, which makes better sense. The veracity of legally admissible evidence must be established by two witnesses. If a document is brought into court signed by two witnesses, the witnesses share equally the responsibility for the evidence contained in the document. Here, one of the two witnesses to the document, X, is unknown to his fellow, Y. If Y attests to his own signature, then he bears one-half responsibility for the evidence, the most he is permitted. The question is, may Y then join himself with Z, a third party "from the street," to attest to the signature of X, who is absent? If so, more than half of the evidence would be dependent upon Y.

27. That is, Y and Z may not join together to attest the signature of X, providing the required two witnesses, since three-quarters of the evidence would be dependent upon Y, and if Y were found unfit, only one-quarter would be left.

28. Or "knows him."

29. Y, whose handwriting everyone knows, was signatory to a document and is now present and able to attest to his signature. X, the other signatory, is not present and only Y recognizes X's handwriting. Since others recognize and can attest to Y's signature, making it unnecessary for him to attest to his own, may he be viewed as if he were a thirty party "from the street," to be joined with Z, another "from the street," in attesting to the signature of X? Then he would only bear one-half responsibility for the evidence, and one witness would be relied upon like two. Or, since Y is present, and since the sages teach in Mishnah Ketubot 2:4, that a person is believed to say, "this is my handwriting," no one else is needed to testify for Y, yet if Y joins Z in attesting to X, he would bear three-quarters of the responsibility for the evidence.

30. If he needn't attest to his own signature, but only to that of the other signatory.

31. Actually, three-quarters of the evidence. This outcome is impossible.

32. The known Jew.

33. The one unknown to all but his fellow, to attest to his Jewishness.

34. After the known Jew establishes the identity of the other, they both serve as witnesses attesting to something else. The consequence is that the known Jew bears responsibility for three-quarters of the testimony, surely an untenable situation. Here likewise, in the case of attesting to a document or establishing the New Moon, two witnesses must bear equal responsibility.

And here also the result would be that the entire testimony is established by one witness.

7. We learned there:[35] the officer said to them, go and see if the time for slaughtering has come. If it has come, the one who perceives it says "it is daylight." What is "daylight"?[36] Morning star.[37] There they say:[38] "the morning star shines," [which means in Palestinian Aramaic] "the morning star shines."

8. And is [the statement of] one witness sufficient?[39] It is a different case here, for you are (not)[40] able to verify it. But one might be suspicious, saying that while he[41] ascends and descends, the light has come? The thing is recognized.[42]

9. If one witness said: "so and so was born on the Sabbath," they circumcise him on his testimony.[43] Nightfall at the end of the Sabbath—they move him on his testimony.[44] Rabbi Ami moved [the infant] based upon the testimony of the midwives.[45] Rabbi Mattaniah moved [the infant] based upon the light of the moon.[46] Rabbi Ami[47] circumcised based upon the testimony of

35. In Mishnah Yoma 3:1 and Mishnah Tamid 3:2.
36. That is, what does *borqai* mean?
37. *Bareqet*, the source of *borqai*.
38. In Babylonia. The test gives both the Babylonian and Palestinian Aramaic for "the morning star shines."
39. I.e., can the testimony of the one person who perceives the daylight be relied upon?
40. The negative *she'en* appears in the Leiden MS, but it is absent in the Rabennu Ḥananel parallel. In the genizah parallel published by Louis Ginzberg in *Genizah Studies in Memory of Doctor Solomon Schechter*, vol. 1, p. 387, the word *she'en* has been added to the MS in the margin. Ginzberg notes that the word does not belong here, and I concur.
41. Another witness who goes up to check.
42. One can easily tell if the witness lied, since they know what degree of light should be evident by now.
43. That is, circumcise on the eighth day, superseding the Sabbath.
44. If the one witness testifies that the Sabbath is over, this would suffice for the purpose of moving a child born at eight months who cannot be moved on the Sabbath. With regard to the eight-month child, Tos. Shabbat 15:5, b. Shabbat 135a, b. Yebamot 80a, and b. Baba Batra 20a teach that a child born at eight months is on a par with a stone (because he is viewed as nonviable) and may not be moved on the Sabbath.
45. If a midwife were to testify that a baby suspected of being born after eight months of pregnancy had the symptoms of a viable child, that is, fully grown fingernails and hair (Tos. Shabbat. 15:7), this sufficed for Rabbi Ami to move the infant on the Sabbath. The translation "midwives" is based upon the emendation suggested in *The Aruch* and Levy.
46. R. Mattaniah, on his own testimony that night had fallen at the end of the Sabbath, moved a child born at eight months. The translation "the light of the moon" follows *The Aruch* and Levy. According to the Jastrow Dictionary, p. 44, "on the lamplighters' declaring that night had set in."
47. It is likely that R. Imi here and R. Ami mentioned just above are the same person, since the second appearance of the name merely adds a *yod*. In the paral-

women who said that it was still light over Susita.[48]

10. Do those who know the moon-witnesses profane the Sabbath on their behalf?[49] Let us prove it from this: Rabbi N'horai bar Shanyah said,[50] it happened that I went down[51] to testify of a certain witness in Usha, and they didn't need me,[52] but I sought a pretext to visit my fellows.[53]

11. And what disorder occurred there?[54] That they used to say, "the Festival of Weeks [always] follows the Sabbath,"[55] and they used to go out on it while it was still evening with the presumption that it would be sanctified.[56]

12. Henceforth concerning [the New Moon of] Nisan we won't accept them;[57] concerning the rest of the months we should accept them![58] Said Rabbi Jose the son of Rabbi Abun: the essential disordering began with Adar.[59] Henceforth, when there is agreement with them, we should not accept them; but if there is not agreement with them, we may accept them![60] [The

---

lel passage from Yoma, the same two spellings appear, but in the opposite order. Hence I have utilized the name Ami in both cases.

48. In the P'ne Moshe comment on the parallel in Yoma, chapter 3, Halakhah 1, this sentence is explained to mean that R. Ami circumcised on the Sabbath based on the testimony of women who said that the sun could still be seen over the town of Susita on the previous Sabbath when the baby was born.

49. By going to the Bet Din to attest to the credentials of the witnesses.

50. For this name I am following the reading found in the Ginzberg genizah parallel (see footnote 40 above), p. 390.

51. On the Sabbath. This refers to the time period when the Bet Din was located in Usha.

52. Surely they might have found someone in Usha who knew the witness and could testify to his credentials.

53. On the Sabbath in Usha. Hence it was permitted to profane the Sabbath in order to accompany and to attest to a witness.

54. From the actions of the *minim* mentioned in the Mishnah. What follows is the calendar the *minim* were striving to achieve by their manipulations.

55. See b. Menachot 65b.

56. That is, messengers would go out on the evening prior to the day of the thirtieth of Adar, which was a Sabbath, to testify that the moon had been seen, even though it had not been sanctified, so that the first of Nisan would fall on the Sabbath. That way, Passover would fall on the Sabbath, the second day of Passover would fall on Sunday, and the counting of the *Omer* would begin "on the morrow of the Sabbath" to follow the *minims*' literal reading of Lev. 23 : 11, 15. With thirty days in Nisan and twenty-nine days in Iyar, the fiftieth day of the *Omer*, the Festival of Weeks, would also fall on a Sunday.

57. I.e., testimony from anyone who is not known.

58. Testimony from anyone.

59. In order for their calendation to emerge, the *minim* had to manipulate so that the thirtieth of Adar, i.e., the first of Nisan, would fall on the Sabbath.

60. The translation proposed for this sentence follows the emended text found in Rabennu Hananel to Rosh Hashanah 22b. Z.W. Rabinovitz, in *Sha'are Torath Eretz Israel*, p. 274, suggests a similar corrected reading. The translation of the Leiden MS and the printed texts would be as follows: "Henceforth, when there

Mishnah teaches] this because of this.[61]

13. It happened that the Boethusians hired two false witnesses to testify concerning the moon that it had been sanctified. The one came, gave his testimony, and went on his way. The other came and said: I was going up the ascent of Adumim and I saw it, crouching between two rocks, its head like [that of] a calf, its ears like [those of] a kid, and I saw it, became frightened, and sprang back. And behold 200 *zuzim* are tied up in my purse. They said to him: behold the 200 *zuzim* are given to you

(58a) as a gift, and those who sent you shall come to be lashed. As for you, why did you place yourself in such danger? He said to them: I saw them seeking to mislead the Sages. I said [to myself] better that I should go and make it known to the Sages.

14. And what disorder occurred there?[62] That these[63] were lighting beacons on this day, and these[64] were lighting beacons the next day, and they used to think that the Bet Din had changed their mind to intercalate, and they became disordered.

15. Who discontinued the beacon fires? Rabbi[65] discontinued the beacon fires, and he permitted the murderer,[66] and he permitted hearsay testimony,[67] and he permitted that they go out on

---

is agreement with them, we should accept them; if there is not agreement with them, we should not accept them." This version assumes that since the *Bet Din Hagadol* is mathematically able to calculate when the moon will appear, they might then accept or reject testimony from witnesses unknown to them predicated upon agreement of the testimony with their own calculations.

61. The Mishnah teaches that because of the manipulating on the part of the *minim*, the Rabbis decreed that they would only accept testimony from moon-witnesses known to them. Even though they might use their own calculations as an independent check on unknown witnesses, nonetheless such a system might open them to possible error in the case of a false witness. Hence, because of the mishnaic teaching, they completely disregard the testimony of witnesses unknown to them and unattested, even when they don't agree with the Rabbis.

62. The Talmud text has moved on to examine the next part of Mishnah 1, which deals with the Samaritans' sabotage of the beacon system.

63. Authorized by the Bet Din.

64. The Samaritans.

65. According to Rabinovitz, *Sha'are . . .* , p. 275, we learn from R.H. chapter 1, Mishnah 4: "Because of six New Moons the messengers go forth . . . . And while the Temple still existed, they went forth also on Iyar because of the Minor Passover." Hence the system of lighting beacons must have been dropped while the Temple was still standing, and the "Rabbi" here referred to must have been Rabban Gamaliel the Elder. Rabinovitz goes on to prove that *Nasiim* other than Judah Hanasi are referred to in the literature as simply "Rabbi."

66. To testify concerning the moon. Rabinovitz, *Sha'are . . .* , connects this sentence with the following near the beginning of Halakhah 4: "Then Rabban Gamaliel the Elder came and decreed that they might walk two thousand cubits in any direction." He emends *rotseah*, murderer, to read *yetsiah*, going out.

67. Regarding the moon.

it[68] while it was still evening with the presumption that it would be sanctified.[69]

16. Rabbi Abbahu said: even though you say that they discontinued the beacon fires, they didn't discontinue those from the Sea of Tiberias.[70]

17. Rabbi Zeira asked before Rabbi Abbahu: regarding those that we see at Safed, why do they light beacons?[71] He said to him: Rabbi discontinued the beacon fires. So with regard to Safed, why does it light beacons? Only for the sake of declaration that they know.

18. They don't raise up [beacons] the night of its proper time,[72] but rather the night of its intercalation.[73] They don't raise up [beacons] the night of its proper time because of Yom Tov,[74] but they raise them up the night of its intercalation.[75]

19. They don't raise up [beacons] except for the New Moons which are established in their proper time, because of Yom Tov which happens to fall on the Eve of the Sabbath.[76]

20. They don't raise up [beacons] the night of its proper time because of Yom Tov.[74] They don't raise up [beacons] the night of

68. Twilight at the end of day 29 or the night which begins day 30.

69. The next day. For example, the moon is seen clearly at the end of day 29 near nightfall, or at the beginning of day 30 when darkness has set in. Since the assumption is that, come day, it will be declared Rosh Ḥodesh, the messengers depart this previous night in order to hasten their trips.

70. That is, the northernmost signal station, Bet Baltin, which is mentioned in Mishnah 3. Samaritans did not live near there, so there was no fear that the signal-fire system would be sabotaged.

71. Rabinovitz, Sha'are . . . , reads the passage to mean: regarding those who can see [the Sea of Tiberias like Safed]. He indicates that Samaritans were to be found around Safed, and hence the question was raised as to whether beacons could be used where such a possibility for sabotage existed. Rabbi Zeira is suggesting that in places like Safed they use beacons, not to notify another signal station that the New Moon had been proclaimed, but only as a confirmation of the fact that the residents of the town were aware of the New Moon.

72. The night which begins the thirtieth day.

73. The night which begins the thirty-first day, i.e., the night after its sanctification.

74. To assure that the beacon for the thirtieth of Elul will not be lit the evening of Rosh Hashanah, which is forbidden. Rather they would light it after Rosh Hashanah to indicate that Elul had not been intercalated.

75. Tosefta Rosh Hashanah 1 : 17 reads: "When do they kindle flares for the new moon? On the night following its announcement. How so? [If] it coincided with the eve of the Sabbath and the Sabbath, they kindle flares on its account at the end of the Sabbath. And if it came in its proper time, they kindle flares on its account. But if not, they do not kindle flares on its account. On account of all the new moons did they kindle flares" (Jacob Neusner translation, Moed, p. 253).

76. The beacons were used only to indicate the defective months. This way, no confusion would develop when the fire was seen on the Saturday night following a Rosh Hashanah that began on Thursday night. Potentially, the same confu-

its intercalation because of honoring the Sabbath. Now if you say to raise them up whether for the New Moons which are established in their proper time, or whether for intercalated months which are not established in their proper time, if you say thus, they would think perhaps the Bet Din had ruled to intercalate and they become disordered.[77]

Halakhah 2

1. What is *'atse shemen*? Pinewood.[78] Rabbi Jonah said: the torches were moved in the manner of the runner (in zigzag).[79]

2. Rabbi Zeira said:[80] so that they not be thinking it is a star. Rabbi Jose said: we have seen a star go up and down; we have seen a star go and come.

3. It was taught:[81] on the mountains of Mikhvar and Gedor. Rav Huna said: when we went up to here,[82] we ascended to the top of Bet Baltin, and we saw the Babylonian palms as if they were locusts.[83]

---

sion might otherwise also develop in any case where a defective month would end on Thursday evening. In such cases, the beacons were lit on the night which began the thirty-second day.

77. If they were required to kindle beacons on the night which begins day 31 in the case of defective months, or the night which begins day thirty-two in the case of full months, then in the case where Rosh Hashanah falls on Thursday night and Friday, and beacons cannot be lit Friday night because of the Sabbath, they could be lit only on Saturday night to indicate a defective month, the same time when beacons would be lit to indicate a full month. The same problem would arise whenever *Rosh Hodesh* would fall on Thursday night and Friday.

78. Jastrow Dictionary, p. 281. In *Hayerushalmi Kiphshuto*, p. 63, Lieberman notes an emendation of a closely related word and interprets as the woolly substance of cedar twigs which is used for wicks.

79. Jastrow Dictionary, p. 830, under *maqzaza*. The translation that emerges from the P'ne Moshe understanding of the text is different: "What is the meaning of very light olive wood? Rabbi Jonah said: like this *maqzanah.*" Hence P'ne Moshe explains this paragraph as being the definition of one tree in terms of another. The definition of the problematic word *dadinin* as "very light" comes from *The Aruch*, vol. 3, p. 26. P'ne Moshe says that the *maqzanah* is another kind of tree but one that is not *dadinin.*

80. Rabbi Zeira's comment assumes Mishnah 2:2, which reads: "And someone would go up to the top of the hill and set fire to them and wave them to and fro, up and down. . . ."

81. In Tosefta R.H. 1:17 as an addition to the signalling stations mentioned in Mishnah 3.

82. That is, from Babylonia to Palestine.

83. The word for "palm trees" appears in the Leiden MS as a marginal gloss in the right margin by another hand. However, the gloss appears correct, since it appears in the genizah version and in a parallel from Genesis Rabbah 38:8.

Halakhah 3

1. A large courtyard called Bet Ya'azek was in Jerusalem. What is the meaning of Bet Ya'azek? That there they were cultivating[84] the law, as it is written (Isaiah 5:2): *and he levelled it, and cleared it of stones, etc.*

Halakhah 4

1. Formerly they[85] would not budge from there[86] all the day. They later came to consider them like vessels which came from outside the Sabbath limit after dark, which can be moved within a range of four cubits.[87]

2. They later came to consider them like vessels which rested in the courtyard, which can be moved within the courtyard.

3. Then Rabban Gamaliel the Elder came and decreed that they might walk two thousand cubits in any direction.

4. It was taught: [the same limit of two thousand cubits applies] even if one came from beyond the Sabbath boundaries to circumcise an infant.

This Mishnah is according to Rabbi Eleazar. For we learned there:[88] Rabbi Eleazar said moreover, they may cut wood [on the Sabbath] to make charcoal in order to forge an iron implement.[89]

Halakhah 5

How Do They Examine the Witnesses, etc.

1. Rabbi Yohanan said: even the one who is mistaken the most of all does not err in this matter, "in front of the sun or behind the sun?"[90]

84. That is, leveling, clarifying.

85. "They" refers to witnesses to the appearance of a New Moon who went beyond their original Sabbath limit (Erubin 45a, Soncino Talmud, p. 310, n. 7).

86. The very place where they first stationed themselves in the courtyard where the witnesses assembled. They were not even permitted a range of four cubits.

87. As any other person who had gone beyond his Sabbath limit and whose movements are in consequence restricted to four cubits on the Sabbath.

88. Mishnah Shabbat 19:1.

89. Just as the mohel can go beyond the boundary on the Sabbath in order to circumcise, so Rabbi Eleazar says that the preparatory acts of circumcision supersede the Sabbath.

90. A question posed to the witnesses in Mishnah 6. See note 16 there. The

It ought not to read otherwise than concavity [of the moon] in front of the sun, concavity [of the moon] behind the sun.[91]

2. Bar Kapara taught both of them [in his Mishnah]: in front of the sun [or] behind the sun; concavity in front of the sun, concavity behind the sun.[92]

3. Rabbi Yoḥanan said: it is written, *Hamshel and Paḥad are with Him, He makes peace in His high places* (Job 25:2).[93] The sun never saw the concavity of the moon.[94]

4. Rabbi Simon ben Yoḥai taught: since the firmament is of water and the stars are of fire and they dwell together and do not harm each other, therefore *He makes peace in His high places.*

5. Rabbi Abun said: the angel himself is half water and half fire, and he has five [incongruous] features: *and his body was like Tarshish,*[95] *and his face as the appearance of lightning, and his eyes like torches of fire, [and his arms and his feet, like the color of polished copper, and the sound of his words was like the noise of a multitude]* (Daniel 10:6).

6. Rabbi Levi said: no planet ever sees the one which precedes it, but all of them ascend like those who ascend a ladder backward.[96]

---

old moon is west of the sun near the horizon, and it descends before sunset; the new moon is east of the sun above the horizon and is visible after sunset. The examiners in the Mishnah are attempting to determine if a witness erred, seeing the old moon (which is "in front of the sun") and thinking it was the new one. Rabbi Yoḥanan here argues that no one makes that obvious an error, and hence he reinterprets the Mishnah's question.

91. Whether the rim of the moon visible from the earth is concave or convex in relation to the sun. "In front of the sun" means "turned towards" and "behind the sun" means "turned away from."

92. I.e., in his Mishnah version, Bar Kapara taught the Mishnah version and the Gemara version.

93. Literally, "Dominion and fear are with him." Here, however, Hamshel and Paḥad are taken to be opposing angels between whom God makes harmony. In the Pesikta parallel, Hamshel is identified as the angel Michael, and Paḥad as Gabriel.

94. God so ordered "His high places" that the sun was never able to see the concavity, or *blemish*, of the moon. That way the moon would not be embarrassed before the sun, nor the sun be gloating over the lessened stature of the moon.

95. English version, "beryl." Here taken to mean the sea.

96. Jastrow Dictionary p. 361. One who ascends or descends a leaning ladder facing away from it (the opposite from the normal way) would have great difficulty maintaining balance while looking any way other than down.

Another rendering, proposed by Saul Lieberman in his notes to Margulies' text of Lev. Rab., p. 871, is like those who ascend "a winding staircase." He envisions the spiral staircases found in boats at that time, and suggests that those on lower steps cannot see those above them in the spiral. Such a spiral staircase is called a "reversible ladder" because it has no difference between its top and its bottom, and hence could be "reversed."

7. The Holy One blessed be He created 365 windows[97] that the world might use them: 182 in the east, and 182 in the west, and one in the center of the firmament, from which it came forth at the beginning of the Creation.

The distance the sun covers in thirty days, the moon covers in two and a half days. What the sun covers in two months, the moon covers in five days. What the sun covers in three months, the moon covers in seven and a half days. What the sun covers in six months, the moon covers in fifteen days. What the sun covers in twelve months, the moon covers in thirty [days].[98]

8. Rabbi Jonah said: there is not here an [exact] measure, but rather a little less.[99]

9. It was taught: if it [the reflection of the moon] was seen in a reflecting glass or in water, they may not testify concerning it.

10. Rabbi Ḥiyya bar Abba said: if they saw it exit from one cloud and enter into another cloud, they may testify concerning it.

11. It is like this: Rabbi Ḥanina went to En-Tab[100] to the blessing of the New Moon[101] and the weather was cloudy. He said, now they will say: how heavy is the weather of this old man![102] So the Holy One Blessed be He punctured it for him like a sieve, and it appeared through it.

12. Rabbi Ḥiyya the Great walked in the light of the old moon for four miles.[103]

13. Then he started to[104] cast stones at it and he said: don't embarrass the sons of your master. This evening [according to our calculations] we must see you [new] at such and such a place; and you are seen now in this place?! Immediately, [by a miracle] the moon disappeared.

14. To the north of it, to the south of it. Some authorities teach: [if he says] to the north of it, his statement is confirmed.

---

97. Corresponding to the days of the year.
98. This refers to movement through the zodiac.
99. Twenty-nine days, twelve hours, and 793 parts of an hour.
100. A place where the New Moon was proclaimed in the days of Rabbi.
101. Moshe Assis suggested this rendering, emending *lmimna* to *lsimna*, *mem* to *samech*. It is possible that *lsimna* was the original reading, and it was changed by another hand.
102. This is the first time he had come to testify concerning the moon, and scoffers might say he brought the bad weather.
103. On day 29 when they were already hoping to see the New Moon.
104. This follows the emendation suggested by Rabinovitz, *Sha'are* . . . , p. 276, who draws upon parallels in Yebamot, chapter 1, Halakhah 6; Buber Tanḥuma Bo, par. 8, p. 24a; Yalkut Shimoni Bo, section 191, near the beginning of paragraph 2; b. Rosh Hashanah 25a.

Other authorities teach: [if he says] to the south of it, his statement is confirmed.

15. With regard to the one who says "to the north of it his statement is confirmed," from Tevet until Tammuz. With regard to the one who says "to the south of it his statement is confirmed," from Tammuz until Tevet.

16. What was its height [above the horizon]? This one says, a distance equal to one ox-prod. And this one says, a distance equal to two ox-prods. Some authorities teach their statements are confirmed. And other authorities teach: their statements are not confirmed.

17. With regard to the one who says "their statements are confirmed," this is in the case of such witnesses as had been standing [at the time of observation] one above[105] and one below. With regard to the one who says "their statements are not confirmed," this is in the case of such witnesses as had been standing on the same level.

18. What was its width [of crescent]? Like a barley grain or more.[106] And if he said, "in front of the sun," he has not said anything.[107]

Halakhah 6

1. It is taught: Rabbi Simon ben Yoḥai says, *And you shall sanctify the fiftieth year* (Leviticus 25:10). One sanctifies years and not months.

2. But are we not taught, the head of the Bet Din says: "It is sanctified"? What is the meaning of "it is sanctified?" Affirmed.[108]

3. It is taught: for the purpose of sanctifying the moon, they begin [to take votes] from the leader.

4. Said Rabbi Ḥiyya bar Ada: the Mishnah says thus, the head of the Bet Din says "it is sanctified."

5. It is taught: for the purpose of intercalating the year, they begin [to take votes] from the side [bench].[109]

---

105. That is, from on high.
106. That is, very tiny. This interpretation was suggested by Moshe Assis.
107. The meaning of this phrase is problematic.
108. There is no obligation to "sanctify," as there is for the Jubilee year.
109. The junior judges. This is the practice in capital cases. See M. Sanhedrin 4:2.

6. Said Rabbi Z'bida: but regarding that house down there,[110] they don't do it this way.

And they didn't recall what Rabbi Hiyya bar Madya, Rabbi Jonah, Rabbi Abba, Rabbi Hiyya bar Abba[111] in the name of Rabbi Yohanan said: for the purpose of sanctifying the moon, they begin [to take votes] from the leader; for the purpose of intercalating the year, they begin [to take votes] from the side [bench].[109]

7. It happened that Rabbi Yohanan entered, and he was the youngest among them, so they said to him: say [the formula], "behold the year is sanctified through *its* intercalation."[112] He said, behold the year is sanctified through intercalation.[113]

(58b)   8. Rabbi Yonatan[114] said: see the formulation which the smith's son[115] has taught us.[113] If he had said "through its intercalation," I would have said that these are the 11 days that the sun['s year] exceeds the moon['s year] each year. But "through intercalation"—that the sages added to it thirty days and intercalated it.

9. Rabbi Jacob bar Aha [in the name of] Rabbi Jose in the name of Rabbi Yohanan: to proclaim an intercalation, we go by the dates of ordination,[116] for the Bet Hamidrash, we go by who is usual,[117] assuming that everyone speaks in his place.[118]

10. For example, Rabbi Hanina opens; Rabbi Yohanan and Rabbi Simon ben Lakish close. Rabbi Abba bar Z'bida opens; Rabbi Hiyya and Rabbi Jose and Rabbi Ami close. Rabbi Haggai opens; Rabbi Jonah and Rabbi Jose close.

11. Kahana was ordained prior to Rabbi Jacob bar Aha.

---

110. Rabbi's college.

111. The MS reads "R. Hiyya in the name of R. Hiyya in the name of R. Yohanan . . ." This is clearly in error. Therefore I am suggesting R. Hiyya bar Abba as a possible correct reading.

112. I.e., proclaiming a leap year, inserting a second Adar.

113. Omitting the *heh* with a mapek at the end of the word, in accordance with the reading found in the genizah fragment.

114. Although our MS reads R. Yohanan, parallels from Sanhedrin read R. Yonatan, and I have followed those readings.

115. R. Yohanan.

116. The oldest graduate voting first.

117. I.e., the frequency of a given person's presence. According to P'ne Moshe, the question refers to who opens the academy discussion.

118. Korban Ha'edah sees the question as one of seniority determined by age. P'ne Moshe sees the reference as being to the system of assigned seats in the academy based upon academic ability. Here the *Rosh Yeshivah*, R. Hanina, opens, and R. Yohanan and R. Simon ben Levi close and answer after him, and then come the others in their assigned order.

Rabbi Jacob bar Aha entered before him for the intercalation [of the year]. He[119] said, So! The author of the rule does not maintain it![120]

12. Rabbi Hiyya bar Abba was standing in prayer. Rabbi Kahana entered and stood in prayer behind him. When Rabbi Hiyya bar Abba finished his prayers, he sat down, so as not to pass before Rabbi Kahana, [who was extending his prayers].[121] When Rabbi Kahana finished, he[122] said to him: "Is that your custom, to annoy your superiors?"

He[123] said to him: Rabbi, I am of the house of Eli, and it is written concerning the house of Eli: *that the iniquity of Eli's house shall not be purged with sacrifice nor offering forever* (1 Samuel 3:14). "With sacrifice and with offering" atonement is not made for him; but with prayer atonement is made for him.

So he[122] prayed concerning him[123] and he[123] had the good fortune to grow old until his fingernails became red like a baby.[124]

13. It happened concerning Rabbi Simon ben Lakesh that they let an old man go before him for the purpose of intercalation [of the year],[125] and they brought him in from their gate.[126] Said [Rabbi Simon ben Lakesh]: such may be their reward!

14. But he didn't recall that Rabbi Krispa said in the name of Rabbi Yohanan: it happened that three cowherds intercalated the year. One of them said: the early and the late seeds bloom simultaneously in Adar.[127] And another said: When an East wind is in Adar, blow up your cheek and expel to meet it.[128] And another said: an ox in Adar in its pen will die,[129] and in the shade of a fig

119. Kahana.
120. Above, it was Jacob bar Aha himself in the name of Rabbi Yohanan who said that with regard to intercalation of the year, one goes by the dates of ordination. Here he isn't fulfilling his own words!
121. It is forbidden to pass before someone in the midst of prayers. The knowledge that Rav Kahana was extending his prayers comes from a parallel text in Sanhedrin.
122. R. Hiyya.
123. R. Kahana.
124. I.e., he lived to an old age.
125. Although the man was not entitled to precede R. Simon ben Lakesh, since he was an inconsequential individual pressed into service from the market place.
126. Jastrow, under *halah* on p. 352, translates: "So they removed him from this court session and for all future ones." This is wrong.
127. If the wheat sown early and the barley sown later sprout together, it is Adar, since it is obviously warm enough. If not, it is Shevat.
128. According to Jastrow, *yapah*, p. 586, if a person feels the warmth of thy breath blown against the East wind, such is Adar, and no Adar Sheni is to be intercalated. Another possibility is that the force of the winter wind has so spent itself that one's breath is as strong as the wind.
129. Because of the cold of the morning or night. Jastrow, under 'adrah,

tree it scratches its hide.[130] We saw a year without any of them, and the year was intercalated on their say-so.[131]

15. Rabbi Ḥelbo said: and the Bet Din agreed with them.[132] But did not Rabbi Zeira say: provided that all of them decide from one [and the same] reason? Since these agree with these, and these agree with these, it is as if all of them decide from one reason.[133]

16. And Rabbi Simon ben Lakesh became angry concerning this matter. He was troubled because of what Rabbi Eleazar said, for Rabbi Eleazar said: *And my hand shall be against the prophets that see falsehood, and that divine lies; they shall not be in the secret council of my people, [and they shall not be written in the register of the house of Israel, and they shall not come into the land of Israel]* (Ezekiel 13:9). *[They shall not be in the secret council of my people]*—that refers to the "secret of intercalation." *And they shall not be written in the register of the house of Israel*—that refers to ordination. *And they shall not come into the land of Israel*—that refers to the land of Israel.

17. And Rabbi Eleazar said: when I went up to here,[134] I said, "here it is" with regard to one;[135] when I was ordained, I said, "here it is" with regard to two;[136] when I went up for intercalation [to be on the council], I said, "here it is" with regard to three.[137]

18. Rabbi Abba bar Z'bida in the name of Rav: the reasoning of Rabbi Eleazar the son of Rabbi Zadok[138] is that since the heavenly Bet Din sees that the earthly Bet Din is not sanctifying it, they sanctify it.[139]

---

p. 1046. Another possible translation for *'adrah* is "herd" instead of "pen."

130. At midday, the animal wants to be in the shade because the sun is hot.

131. The purpose of intercalation is to readjust the seasons, so that the second Adar has the climate of the first Adar in normal years.

132. With the three cowherds.

133. I.e., there are no disagreements.

134. To the land of Israel.

135. Another possible translation: "here (it has been fulfilled with regard) to me." He is proclaiming that he has successfully overcome the first of the three prohibitions of Ez. 13:9—"they shall not come into the land of Israel."

136. The second prohibition of Ez. 13:9—"they shall not be written in the register of the house of Israel," which R. Eleazar takes to be ordination.

137. The third prohibition of Ez. 13:9—"they shall not be in the secret council of my people," which R. Eleazar takes to be the council that decides on intercalation.

138. The Gemara text of the Leiden MS here, the end of Mishnah 2:8, and a parallel from Leiden Sanhedrin, chapter 1, Halakhah 2, all read R. Eleazar of the school of R. Zadok. The Mischnacodex Kaufmann does also. The Mishnah edited by Lowe reads R. Eleazar son of R. Zadok, and this is the correct reading for the name of this fourth generation Tanna.

139. This comment is on the end of Mishnah 2:8, "if it is not seen in its

Halakhah 7

1. Rabbi Simlai said: the reasoning of Rabbi Yoḥanan ben Nuri[140] is that concerning any new moon born before six hours,[141] there is not the power in the eye to see the old moon.[142]

2. And it is taught thus: if the old moon appears in the morning, the new moon doesn't appear in the evening; if the new moon appears in the evening, the old moon could not have appeared in the morning.

3. Said Rabbi Ḥiyya bar Abba: so why did Rabban Gamaliel accept them? For thus was a tradition he had from his fathers: sometimes it goes by the short route,[143] sometimes by the long route.

Halakhah 8

1. To whom did he send?[144] From that which is taught: Rabbi Joshua said, it would have been better for me to lie [dead] on the bed, Rabban Gamaliel not having sent this thing. This indicates that it was sent to Rabbi Joshua.

2. At the hand of whom was it sent? From that which is taught in these words: he said to him, you have comforted me, Akiba. This indicates that it was sent at the hand of Rabbi Akiba.

3. What did he [Akiba] have to teach?[145] Rabbi Jose said: we know that if they sanctified without witnesses, it is still sanctified. So what did he come to attest? That if they sanctified it and afterwards the witnesses were found to be lying,[146] behold this is a valid act of sanctification.[147]

---

proper time, they do not proclaim it sanctified, because heaven has already sanctified it" [at the beginning of day 31].

140. In Mishnah 9, R. Yoḥanan responded to the witnesses who said "we saw it in the morning in the east and in the evening in the west" by calling them false witnesses.

141. I.e., noon.

142. According to Korban Haʿedah, six hours before the *molad* it is impossible to see the old moon because of its smallness, and likewise six hours after the *molad* it is impossible to see the new moon because of its smallness. Thus R. Yoḥanan ben Nuri called them false witnesses.

143. Sometimes it hurries quickly without a twelve-hour period when it cannot be seen.

144. Mishnah 11 begins, "Rabban Gamaliel sent to him." From the Mishnah text itself, one cannot tell whether the antecedent to "him" is R. Yoḥanan in Mishnah 9 or R. Joshua in Mishnah 10. We rule out R. Dosa since in Mishnah 12 the person in question goes to R. Dosa.

145. In Mishnah 11, Akiba's teaching is not explicitly stated.

146. That is, other witnesses came to discredit their testimony.

147. This is apparently a paraphrase of Tosefta 2:1, which reads: "[If] they

4. But behold have we not been taught:[148] "once more than forty pairs [of witnesses] were passing [through], and Rabbi Akiba detained them in Lod." That is because there were forty pairs, but if it had been one pair, he wouldn't have detained it.[149]

Halakhah 9

1. It is written *[and Samuel said to the people,] it is the Lord who advanced Moses and Aaron and brought your fathers up out of the land of Egypt . . .* (1 Samuel 12:6) *and the Lord sent* Jerubbaal *and* Bedan, *and* Jephthah, *and* Samuel *[and delivered you out of the hand of your enemies on every side, and you dwelt in safety]* (v. 11). Jerubbaal—that is Gideon.[150] Bedan—that is Samson.[151] Jephthah—that is Jephthah the Gileadi.[152]

The text compared these three lightweights of the world [Jerubbaal, Bedan, and Jephthah] to the three mighty ones of the world [Moses, Aaron, and Samuel] to teach you that the courts of Gideon and of Jephthah and of Samson were equal to those of Moses, Aaron, and Samuel.[153]

---

sanctified the new moon at the proper time, but the witnesses concerning it turned out to be deceitful, lo, this is a valid act of sanctification" (Neusner translation). In Siphra Emor 10:2, the statement from the Tosefta is supported by the proof-text Lev. 23:4, which we find in R. Akiba's name in Mishnah 2:11.

148. In Mishnah 1:7.

149. That is, the pair. The case is that forty pairs of witnesses were profaning the Sabbath to go to Yavneh. Akiba stopped them from the unnecessary profanation. If there were one couple, however, he would not have stopped them, according to the Palestinian Talmud's interpretation.

The incident of the forty pairs of witnesses is from Mishnah R.H. 1:7. There R. Akiba detains them, preventing an unnecessary profanation. Rabban Gamaliel disagrees, fearing that to detain this group will merely discourage them from going to testify in the future. The P.T. origin of this sugya is Megillah, chapter 2, Halakhah 7. There we find a general principle stated by R. Akiba that any work which can be done prior to the Sabbath does not supersede the Sabbath; any work which cannot possibly be done prior to the Sabbath supersedes the Sabbath. The example is then cited of R. Akiba detaining the forty pairs of witnesses in Lod on the Sabbath. If, however, there had been but one pair, the Talmud speculates that he would not have detained them, because the need to testify concerning the moon supersedes the Sabbath.

Rabinovitz, *Sha'are . . .* , p. 276, suggests that this incident of the forty pairs of witnesses should not have been transferred here from its context in Megillah, since it does not belong here.

150. Judges 6:32 says with regard to Gideon: *and the people called him on that day Jerubbaal, saying, let Baal contend against him, because he has overthrown his altar.*

151. Who came from Dan.

152. Judges, chapter 11. Jephthah conquered the Ammonites.

153. The implicit question being addressed is why these "lightweight" judges, rather than one like Joshua.

2. And not only this, but it juxtaposes the great men from either side, and the lesser ones in the middle.[154]

3. Rabban Gamaliel arose and kissed him on his head and said to him: come in peace, my teacher and my disciple. "My teacher" in wisdom, "my disciple" in fear of sin. "My teacher" in wisdom "and my disciple" in that all that I decree upon him, he fulfills.

4. It is written: *Whose oxen are well laden; [with no breach, and no going forth, and no complaining in the streets]* (Psalms 144:14). A dispute between Rabbi Yoḥanan and Rabbi Simon ben Lakesh. Rabbi Yoḥanan said: laden oxen isn't written here, but our [laden] teachers—in Torah.[155] "Laden"—when the great bear the small,[156] "there is no breach, nor going forth; there is no complaining in the streets."

5. Rabbi Simon ben Lakesh interprets this verse just in a reverse way [to Rabbi Yoḥanan's interpretation]: laden oxen isn't written here, but our teachers are borne with, when the small bear the great,[157] "then there is no breach, nor going forth; there is no complaining in the streets."

6. Rabbi Shila of the village of T'marta in the name of Rabbi Yoḥanan: *He appointed the moon for seasons; the sun knows its coming* (Psalms 104:19). From the sun "one knows its coming," *He appointed the moon for festivals* (Psalms 104:19).

7. Said Rabbi Berakia, it is written: *and they departed from Rameses in the first month, [on the fifteenth day of the first month; on the morrow after the passover the children of Israel went up out of Egypt . . .]* (Numbers 33:3). When it sets on the night of the festival, fourteen sunsets are in it;[158] hence from the setting of the sun, you count for the moon.

8. Said Rabbi Simon: and let them be [for signs, and for seasons, and for years, and for days] (Genesis 1:14)—by means of that [sun] and by means of that [moon].

9. Rabbi Yoḥanan said: *And it was evening, and it was morning, one day* (Genesis 1:5).[159]

154. I.e., Samuel is at the end of the combined verses of 1 Sam. 12:6 and 11, not after Moses and Aaron, as he should be in the order of importance.
155. The point of the d'rash, according to Korban Ha'edah, is that since it says *alufenu* instead of *alufim*, it couldn't be talking about animals, because one's own animals would not injure their masters since they know them, but this would not be the case regarding others. Here it means teachers instead.
156. That is, sustain, maintain, carry the burden and the responsibility.
157. That is, accept their leadership and acknowledge their superiority.
158. That is, the month.
159. Proof that a day begins with sundown the previous evening and continues until the following sundown.

10. Rabbi Simon ben Lakesh said: *This month [shall be to you the beginning of months]* (Exodus 12:2)—when all of it [the day] will be from the new [month].[160]

11. You must say, therefore, that what Rabbi Yohanan said is necessary for Rabbi Simon ben Lakesh, and what Rabbi Simon ben Lakesh said is necessary for Rabbi Yohanan. If Rabbi Yohanan made his statement, but Rabbi Simon ben Lakesh did not make his statement, we would have to admit that it didn't even say all of it [the day] must be from the new [month].[161] This proves that there is a need for what Rabbi Simon ben Lakesh said.

Or if Rabbi Simon ben Lakesh made his statement, but Rabbi Yohanan did not make his statement, we would have to admit that it only said day,[162] but not night. This proves that there is a need for what Rabbi Yohanan said, and a need for what Rabbi Simon ben Lakesh said.

---

160. That is, the entire day including the previous evening must be from the new month if the day is to be sanctified.

161. I.e., not necessarily establishing that the entire day (evening and day) must be from the new month. According to Korban Ha'edah, we do learn not to put evening in the old month and morning in the new month. Both are either in the old or the new month, following the reasoning of R. Yohanan.

What we don't learn from R. Yohanan is not to consider the day from the new month if part of it is from the old month.

162. Actual day.

3 Mishnah Rosh Hashanah Chapter Three

(58c) 1. If the Court and all Israel had seen it,[1] if the witnesses had been examined,[2] but there was no time to say "it is sanctified" before it grew dark,[3] behold this is an intercalated month.[4]

If the Court alone saw it,[1] let two of them stand up and testify before them,[5] and then they should say: "it is sanctified, it is sanctified!"

If three who themselves constitute the Court saw it,[1] let two of them stand up, and let them seat some of their colleagues with the remaining judge, and they[6] testify before them,[7] and they[7] should say: "it is sanctified, it is sanctified"; for an individual is not regarded as trustworthy by himself.[8]

2. All shofars are valid except for that of a cow, because it is a "horn." Said Rabbi Jose: but are not all shofars called "horn"? For it is said, *and it shall come to pass, that when they make a*

1. That is, the New Moon on the night which begins the thirtieth day.
2. Having arrived on the thirtieth day. Babli R.H. 25b questions the relationship between the first and second phrases: "But when once it has been stated 'If the Court and all Israel had seen it,' why should it further say, 'if the witnesses had been examined'? (i.e., what function do the witnesses serve if the people have seen it?). What it means is, 'or if the witnesses had been examined. . . .'"
3. On the night which begins the thirty-first day.
4. Despite the fact that the Court and all Israel had seen the New Moon on the night of the thirtieth day, and hence the matter was known, despite the fact that the appearance of the New Moon on the thirtieth day had been confirmed through the successful examination of witnesses, nonetheless the month is intercalated because the Court did not sanctify the New Moon in time.
5. Both Korban Ha'edah and P'ne Moshe comment that this paragraph must be referring to a court of twenty-three members.
6. The two former court members turned witness.
7. The newly constituted court of three.
8. For the purpose of proclaiming the sanctification of the New Moon. Rather a minimum court of three is required.

long blast with the ram's horn, when you hear the sound of the shofar (Joshua 6:5).

The shofar[9] for the New Year[10] is from a wild goat, it is straight, and its mouth is overlaid with gold. And two trumpets are on the sides. The shofar is sounded for a long note, and the trumpets are sounded for a short note; for the religious precept of the day concerns the shofar.

3. On fast days they are from rams, curved, and its mouth is overlaid with silver. And two trumpets are between them. The shofar is sounded for a short note, and the trumpets are sounded for a long note; for the religious precept of the day concerns the trumpets.

4. The Jubilee Year is equivalent to the New Year with regard to the blowing of the shofar and the blessings.

Rabbi Judah says: on the New Year they sound those of rams, and at the Jubilee Year those of wild goats.

5. A shofar which was split and which one stuck back together is invalid. If one stuck back together pieces of shofars, it is invalid. If it was perforated and one plugged the hole: if [the plugged hole] affects the blowing, it is invalid; and if not, valid.

6. Regarding one who sounds the shofar into a well, a cellar, or a large jar: if one heard the sound of the shofar, he has fulfilled his obligation; if one heard an echo, he has not fulfilled his obligation. And so too, regarding one who was passing behind the synagogue, or whose house was near the synagogue, and he heard the sound of the shofar, or the sound of the reading of the Scroll of Esther: if he paid attention, he has fulfilled his obligation; and if not, he has not fulfilled his obligation. [This is the rule] even though this one heard and that one heard, for this one paid attention, but that one did not pay attention.

7. *Now it happened that when Moses held up his hand, Israel prevailed [and when he let his hand fall, Amalek prevailed]* (Exodus 17:11). And do the hands of Moses either make or stop war? Rather [the meaning of the verse is] so long as Israel were looking upward and directing their heart towards their Father in heaven, they prevailed; and if not, they would fall.

8. Similarly *God said to Moses: make yourself a venemous serpent and set it upon a pole [and it shall come to pass that everyone who is bitten, when he sees it, shall live]* (Numbers

9. Used in the Temple.
10. In Tishri.

21:8). And does the serpent either kill or sustain life? Rather [the meaning of the verse is] so long as Israel were looking upward and submitting their heart to their Father in heaven, they were healed; and if not, they would pine away.

9. [The shofar blasts of] a deaf-mute, a fool, and a minor do not fulfill the obligations on behalf of the community. This is the general principle: anyone who is not obligated to carry out a particular deed cannot fulfill the obligations on behalf of the community.

Halakhah 1

Gemara. 1. If the Court and all Israel had seen it, etc. So is the Mishnah to be read, "either the Court or all Israel." [11]

2. Rabbi Zeira [in the name of] Rabbi Ami in the name of Rabbi Joshua ben Levi: we may disregard the sighted [New Moon] [12] to intercalate; [13] we may not proclaim the first day of the new month [14] when the New Moon has not been seen.

3. Rabbi Abba [in the name of] Rabbi Ḥiyya in the name of Rabbi Joshua ben Levi: we may proclaim the first day of the new month [14] when the New Moon has not been seen; but we may not disregard the sighted [New Moon] [12] to intercalate.

4. A *baraita* differs from Rabbi Zeira: if the Court and all Israel had seen it, if the witnesses had been examined, but there was no time to say "it is sanctified" before it grew dark, behold this is an intercalated month [15]—because it grew dark. But if it did not grow dark, no! This [16] proves that we may not disregard the sighted [New Moon] [12] to intercalate.

---

11. According to Mishnah 3:1, if the court of twenty-three or of three saw the New Moon, two of them turn witness, and the moon is sanctified; no other witnesses are required. Mishnah, chapter 2, describes in detail the procedure by which the Court accepts testimony from witnesses from among "all Israel" who claim to have seen the New Moon. Hence the Mishnah cannot possibly mean, "If the Court *and* all Israel had seen it," since either separately would suffice for purpose of testimony leading to sanctification. Thus the emendation, "either the Court or all Israel."

12. On the night of the thirtieth day of the month.

13. That is, we may ignore the testimony, or perhaps use delaying tactics so as not to announce the new month before dark.

14. On the thirtieth day.

15. The Leiden MS reads "behold it is sanctified." I have corrected the text in accordance with the Mishnah.

16. The fact that only darkness serves to prevent the announcement of the new month on the thirtieth day.

5. A *baraita* differs from Rabbi Abba: one might think that if it is necessary to add two days, they add two days? Scripture says "day"[17]—one day only. This proves that we may disregard the sighted [New Moon][12] to intercalate.[18]

6. A *baraita* differs from Rabbi Abba: one might think that just as they intercalate the year out of necessity,[19] so likewise they sanctify the New Moon out of necessity?[20] Scripture says, *the New Moon* (Exodus 12:2)—they decide based upon the New Moon. This proves that we may not proclaim the first day of the new month[14] when the New Moon has not been seen.

7. A *baraita* differs from Rabbi Zeira:[21] one might think that if the moon did not appear for two days, thus they would announce the new month after two days? Scripture says, *[speak unto the children of Israel, and say unto them: the appointed seasons of the Eternal which you shall proclaim]* them— [Scripture goes on to emphasize] *these are they [My appointed seasons]* (Leviticus 23:2) and not "these are My appointed sea-

17. The Leiden MS reads *oto*, but from the parallel passages in Tosefta 2:2 and Siphra Emor, chapter 10, we see that the proper reading must be *yom*—day. P'ne Moshe, endorsing this emendation, gives Num. 29:1 as the reference for *yom*, because the verse refers to the first day of the seventh month as a day of blowing the trumpets. He derives from the singular *yom* that one day is the most that can be added for intercalation.

Korban Ha'edah also endorses the emendation from *oto* to *yom*, but gives Lev. 23:6 (as does the Liberman Tosefta) as the proof-text: *And on the fifteenth day (yom) of the same month is the feast of unleavened bread. . . .* He comments that the word *yom* is superfluous, and hence it comes to teach that they could intercalate by *yom eḥad*, or one day, but not more.

The Zuckermandel Tosefta cites Ex. 12:18 for "yom": *In the first [month], on the fourteenth day (yom) of the month in the evening, you shall eat unleavened bread.* Here again the reasoning of Korban Ha'edah above applies: *yom laḥodesh*—intercalate by one day, but not more. Eugene Mihaly supports the assignment of the Exodus 12 proof-text by noting that in the next paragraph, paragraph 6, the proof-text is from Exodus 12:2.

18. The text reads as follows: "This proves that we may not proclaim the first day of the new month when the New Moon has not been seen." However this makes no sense in the context of the argument, and I have followed the reading suggested by Rabinovitz, *Sha'are* . . . , p. 277.

The Mechilta D'Rabbi Ishmael, Horowitz-Rabin edition, p. 8, lines 11–13, also takes up the question of how many days can be intercalated into a month. "Just as what is intercalated into the year is 1/12 thereof, so also what is intercalated into the month should be 1/12 thereof. But Scripture says: *And on the fifteenth day of this month shall be a feast* (Lev. 23:6, Num. 28:17). This teaches that it is only a day that you may intercalate into the month and not 1/12 of the month."

19. To bring the lunar year into seasonal agreement with the solar.

20. To cause holidays and festivals to fall on the proper days.

21. The text for this paragraph says that a *baraita* differs from R. Abba, but I have followed the textual emendation suggested by Rabinovitz, *Sha'are* . . . , p. 277, in substituting R. Zeira.

sons."[22] This is because it did not appear.[23] But if it appeared, no![24] This proves that we may not disregard the sighted [New Moon][12] to intercalate.[25]

8. They [the members of the academy] were able to say: and there is no contradiction; what Rabbi Zeira said concerns the rest of the months; what Rabbi Abba said concerns Nisan and Tishri.[26]

9. Rabbi says: Nisan was never intercalated.[27]

10. But are we not taught [in a Mishnah]:[28] "If the New Moon came in due time . . . ?"[29] *If* it came; [in fact] it did not come [at any time other than its due time].

11. Rav said: Tishri was never intercalated. But are we not

22. The use of the proof-text focuses upon the fact that it contains two superfluous words: (1) (you shall proclaim) *them* (*otam*) and (2) [these are] they (*hem*), with *hem* taking *otam* as its antecedent. Thus, although the verse might have read "these are My appointed seasons," instead it reads "these are *they*, My appointed seasons," with the additional word "they" referring back to "them." "Them" is a demonstrative pronoun, here singling out days 30 and 31 as the only possible ones upon which they might proclaim the first day of the new month. I am grateful to Eugene Mihaly for this interpretation.

23. On the night of the thirtieth of the month, and hence the month was intercalated.

24. If it had been seen at its proper time on the night of the thirtieth day, announcement of the first day of the new month would have been predicated upon the testimony of the witnesses and no other considerations.

25. In the text, this paragraph ends as follows: "This proves that we may not proclaim the first day of the new month when the New Moon has not been seen." My reading follows an emendation by Rabinovitz, *Sha'are* . . . , p. 277.

26. Since the festivals are dependent upon the New Moons of these months, they are sanctified according to necessity.

27. That is, the New Moon Day of Nisan was never fixed on the thirty-first day of Adar. This serves to support the application of R. Abba's statement to Nisan, since he said that "we may proclaim the first day of the new month[14] when the New Moon has not been seen; but we may not disregard the sighted [New Moon] to intercalate." In either case, the result is a defective month.

28. Shekalim 4:5.

29. Mishnah Shekalim 4:5 teaches that each day half a mina of incense was offered morning and afternoon. Since a tradition was received from Moses at Sinai that 368 minas of incense should be prepared each year, ordinary lunar years (354 days plus 3 extra minas for Yom Kippur) would show a surplus and leap years (384) a shortfall. The Mishnah proposes a method for carrying over an ordinary year's surplus without violating Tosefta Rosh Hashanah 1:1 and 1:4, that from *Rosh Hodesh* Nisan on, one must offer incense purchased with the new heave-offering of the shekels. They would set aside from the surplus incense the equivalent of the salaries of the craftsmen who compounded the incense and pay them in incense. Then they would buy the incense back from the craftsmen. If the New Moon came in due time (30th of Adar), they repurchased the incense, as would be the case with any public offering, with the new heave-offering of the shekels. If not (causing Adar to be intercalated), they repurchased the incense with the old shekels. The Gemara is stressing the fact that the Mishnah says "*if* the New Moon came"—the implication being that Adar could be either twentynine or thirty days long.

taught [in a Mishnah]:[30] "If the month [of Tishri] was intercalated . . . ?"[31] *If* it was; [in fact] it was not.

13. Now when they sanctified the year in Usha, on the first
day Rabbi Ishmael the son of Rabbi Yoḥanan ben Baroqah
passed [before the ark] and said it in accord with the view of
Rabbi Yoḥanan ben Nuri.[32] Said Rabban Simon ben Gamaliel:
"That was not the custom which we followed in Yavneh." So on
the second day Rabbi Ḥanina the son of Rabbi Jose the Galilean
passed [before the ark] and said it in accordance with the opinion of Rabbi Akiba.[33] Then said Rabban Simon ben Gamaliel:
"Now that was the custom which we followed in Yavneh."

But have we not been taught that they sanctified it on the first
and the second?

14. Rabbi Zeira said in the name of Rav Ḥisda: that year was
disarranged.[34]

15. What does "on the first" mean? What does "on the second" mean? Rabbi Abba in the name of Rav: the first year and
the second year.[35]

But have we not been taught,[36] "on the first *day*" and "on the
second *day*"?[37]

Tosefta Rosh Hashanah 1 : 1 teaches that Nisan is the New Year for the
heave-offerings of the shekels; 1 : 4 explains how this is to be understood. All
public offerings are offered on the first of Nisan. If the New Moon came in due
time (the 30th of Adar), they make their public offerings from those purchased
with the new heave-offering of the shekels. If it was not seen on the thirtieth,
they make their public offerings on the thirtieth from those purchased with the
old heave-offering, the following day becomes *Rosh Ḥodesh* Nisan, and the
month has been intercalated, contrary to what Rabbi said. The Gemara is stressing the fact that the Tosefta says "*if* the New Moon came"—the implication
being that Adar could be either twenty-nine or thirty days long.
    30. Shevi'it 10 : 2.
    31. The Mishnah deals with a case where a man slaughtered a heifer and di-
vided it among various buyers on what he thought was the first day of the eighth
year. If Tishri were then intercalated, making the day of the sale the last day of
the seventh year, the debt of the buyers would be cancelled; if it were not intercalated, the debt would be valid. The Gemara is stressing the fact that the Mishnah says "*if* the month was intercalated"—the implication being that the New
Moon Day of Tishri could be either on the first day (thirtieth of Elul) or on the
second (thirty-first of Elul).
    32. See Mishnah Rosh Hashanah 4 : 5.
    33. It appears that at this time in Usha they were observing Rosh Hashanah
for two days, the thirtieth and the thirty-first days after the first of Elul. This
would contradict Rav's statement above that "Tishri was never intercalated."
    34. And hence should not be taken as a precedent.
    35. In the first year R. Yoḥanan led the service according to the view of R.
Yoḥanan ben Nuri. In the second year R. Ḥanina led the service according to the
view of R. Akiba.
    36. Tosefta Rosh Hashanah 2 : 11 and above in our text.
    37. Hence the instance cited happened in one year, and either we accept R.

16. If they declared it sanctified before its proper time, or one day after its intercalation; one might think that it ought to be deemed sanctified? Scripture says, *[These are the appointed seasons of the Eternal . . . which you shall proclaim]* them *[in their appointed season]* (Leviticus 23:4); *[speak unto the children of Israel, and say unto them: the appointed seasons of the Eternal which you shall proclaim]* them—[Scripture goes on to emphasize] *these are they My appointed seasons* (Leviticus 23:2) and not "these are My appointed seasons."[38] Before its proper time—the twenty-ninth day; after its intercalation—the thirty-second day.

17. How do we know scripturally that they intercalate the year because of exiles[39] who ascended [towards Jerusalem] but have not yet arrived? Scripture says, *[speak to] the children of Israel [and say to them, concerning the appointed seasons of the Eternal, you shall proclaim them to be holy convocations; these are] my appointed seasons* (Leviticus 23:2). Fix the appointed seasons so that *all* Israel may observe them.

18. Said Rabbi Samuel bar Naḥman: and behold this is the case when they have reached as far as the Euphrates River.

19. Rabbi Jacob Bar Aḥa [in the name of] Rabbi Ami in the name of Rabbi Judah bar Pazzi: if they sanctified it[40] and afterwards the witnesses were found to be lying, behold this is a valid act of sanctification.

20. Rabbi Jose rose with Rabbi Judah bar Pazzi. He said to him: did you hear this thing from your father? He said to him: This is what my Father said in the name of Rabbi Yoḥanan: they do not minutely examine testimony with regard to the New Moon.

Zeira's explanation that the year was disarranged or else we acknowledge that Tishri was intercalated. Rabinovitz, *Shaʾare* . . . , in his comment on the parallel passage in Shevïit, chapter 10, Halakhah 2 (p. 78), somewhat reorders and changes the passage. He suggests the following reading:

Then said Rabban Simon ben Gamaliel: Now that was the custom which we followed in Yavneh. R. Abba in the name of Rav: What does "on the first" mean and what does "on the second" mean? The first year and the second year. But have we not been taught that they sanctified it on the first day and on the second day? R. Zeira said in the name of Rav Ḥisda: that year was disarranged. If they declared it sanctified before the proper time, etc.

38. See footnote 22 to paragraph 7 above.
39. The reference is to pilgrims from the Diaspora who were journeying to Jerusalem for the Passover festival. If the year was not intercalated by adding a second Adar, these pilgrims would not arrive in time.
40. The New Moon.

21. A court that saw the killer, said: if we see him, we don't recognize him![41] They [nonetheless] did not perform the ceremony, as it is written, *our eyes have not seen*—in any case, and behold they had seen.[42]

22. And with regard to a court which saw the killer [murder], one Tanna teaches: let two arise and testify before them. Another Tanna teaches: let all of them arise and testify in another place.[43]

(58d)

23. Rabbi Judah bar Pazzi in the name of Rabbi Zeira: just as they differ here, so likewise they differ over testimony concerning the New Moon.[44]

24. Let one arise and let one be seated, then let one arise and let one be seated?[45] It is different, for the witness does not become judge.[46]

25. It is like this case: Rav Huna knew evidence concerning a certain man. He[47] went to be judged before him,[48] but he[49] denied him.[47]

26. Rabbi Samuel bar Rav Isaac said to him:[49] knowing that

---

41. According to Korban Ha'edah, at an earlier time, the court had "seen" this killer. However, now they would no longer recognize him. Nonetheless, they do not perform the ceremony whereby the neck of the heifer is broken to atone for the murder whose perpetrator is unknown. See Deut. 21:1–9.

Paragraph 21 appears not to belong here. According to David Goldenberg (*In the Margins of the Yerushalmi*, p. 109), its original location, and that of paragraphs 22 and 23, is in PT Sotah, chapter 9, Halakhah 1. Paragraphs 22 and 23 were transferred here because, as Rabbi Judah comments in paragraph 23, the same tannaitic dispute which exists in paragraph 22 concerning the witnessing procedure when a court has seen a murder is found here in R.H. concerning the witnessing procedure when the court has seen the New Moon. Paragraph 21 should not have been transferred with 22 and 23.

42. If one takes the the formula "our eyes have not seen" (Deut. 21:7) in its most literal sense.

43. The implicit question is whether some of those judges who witnessed a crime may act as witnesses while others serve as judges, or whether no witnesses can serve in the capacity of judges.

44. If the entire court saw it, do two testify before the rest, or need they testify before another court?

45. This questions the procedure in Mishnah R.H. 3:1 whereby two of the three judges are replaced on the court by colleagues so that the two can testify. The text here suggests taking the two witnesses one by one from the court so that only one replacement is necessary to nonetheless maintain the court size at three. And lest one argue that the witness turned judge is disqualified by virtue of the fact that he has seen the moon, the same can be said of the third judge who is not testifying.

46. The differentiation is between the third judge, who didn't testify, and the two who did testify.

47. That man.

48. Rav Huna.

49. His opponent.

Rav Huna is a great man, you denied him?! What if he would go and testify concerning you before another court?

27. Rav Huna said to him:[50] and do they do thusly? He[50] said to him:[48] yes. So Rav Huna withdrew from that case, and went to testify concerning him[49] before another court.[51]

28. If objection was raised against the signatures of the witnesses, against the signatures of the judges;[52] Rabbi Abba in the name of Rav Judah: if one wanted to attest by the signatures of the witnesses, one attests; by the signatures of the judges, one attests.[53] And I[54] say, even by one witness, even by one judge, one attests.[55]

29. During the days of Rabbi Abbahu, they came required to say "go'alenu" (Isaiah 47:4) and they said "g'ulatenu" and he accepted them.[56]

30. During the days of Rabbi Berakia, it happened that they became mute. He said to them: did you hear that the New Moon was sanctified? They nodded their heads, and he accepted them.[57]

50. R. Samuel bar Rav Isaac.

51. The example of Rav Huna serves to support the view that one does not serve as a witness before the court on which one serves.

52. The witnesses to the document sign to attest to the accuracy of its contents. The judges then sign to confirm the validity of the document. The one who is raising the objection is thus claiming that the whole document is a forgery.

53. If the judges before whom the case is brought want to confirm the document either by means of witnesses who confirm the signatures of the witnesses to the document or the signatures of the judges, this is valid. But if the witnesses confirmed the signatures of one witness to the document and one of the confirming judges, this is not valid, since the signatures of witness and judge attest to different things.

54. R. Abba.

55. He takes a lenient position, which finds acceptable the confirmation by witnesses of the signature of one witness to the document and one attesting judge, since the end-result is the confirmation by witnesses of two signatures. In so doing, witness and judge are joined together.

56. Two messengers came from the Court to attest to the fact that the New Moon had been sanctified. To identify themselves, they were supposed to utter the prearranged code-word go'alenu. They erred and instead said g'ulatenu. R. Abbahu nonetheless accepted their word, showing a certain acceptable imprecision and flexibility regarding information concerning the moon which would not be allowed in other cases.

The code-word go'alenu (our redeemer) was chosen because just as the moon was covered and then revealed, so likewise will Israel, now covered (dispersed among the nations), shine forth and be redeemed in the future.

57. Here the messengers from the Court could not even approximate the code-word, since they had somehow become mute. R. Berakia had no way to examine them for credibility, and he even had to prompt them as to their mission. Nonetheless he accepted their nods as sufficient indication, thus demonstrating that the role of the messengers was in large measure a formality in any case.

Halakhah 2

1. Some wanted to say: and they do not differ.[58]

2. You find a *baraita* that teaches: Rabbi Jose permits that of a cow, and the sages forbid.

3. What is the reason of Rabbi Jose? *And it shall come to pass, that when they make a long blast with the ram's horn . . .* (Joshua 6:5).[59] What is the reason of the Rabbis?[60] *And it shall please the Lord better than a bullock that has horns and hoofs* (Psalms 69:32). "*Makrn*" is written.[61]

4. And the Rabbis [say]: all shofars are called "*karen*" (horn) and "shofar," except for that of a cow, which is called "*karen*" but is not called "shofar."

5. They raised an objection: behold that of a wild goat is called neither "*karen*" nor "shofar."[62]

6. How is it now?[63] It is like that which Rabbi Levi said: it is different, for the prosecutor is not made the advocate.[64]

Halakhah 3

1. Said Rabbi Jonah: in order that they should straighten their heart in repentance.[65]

2. "Its mouthpiece overlaid with gold:" if they overlaid gold inside, it is invalid. Outside, valid.

3. If they overlaid the spot where the mouth is placed, or if its sound is thick because of the overlay, it is invalid.

---

58. The Rabbis and R. Jose in Mishnah 3:2. Korban Ha'edah suggests as a possible explanation that the Rabbis prohibited the horn of a cow in the very start, whereas R. Jose permitted it only ex post facto.

59. In the previous verse, Joshua 6:4, we find the term *shofrot hayovlim*, literally "trumpets of rams' horns." Then, verse 5 continues: *and it shall come to pass, that when they make a long blast with the ram's horn (karen), when you hear the sound of the* shofar. . . . Hence we see that Scripture equates *karen* and *shofar*.

60. How scripturally do they derive that the horn of the cow is called *karen*?

61. Rabinovitz, *Sha'are . . .* , p. 277, suggests that this comment "'*makrn*' is written" was incorrectly drawn here from Shabbat, chapter 2, Halakhah 3.

62. And yet according to the next Mishnah it is valid.

63. How then do the Rabbis justify their prohibition of the cow's horn?

64. The cow serves as the prosecutor, i.e. poses the case against Israel by virtue of the fact that it serves as a reminder of the golden calf, whereas the shofar serves to elicit the positive memories of Israel, for example, the binding of Isaac.

65. The comment is on the second paragraph of Mishnah 3:2, and it explains why the shofar for the New Year is straight.

4. Said Rabbi Jose: this proves[66] that one who partially hears the plain note of one who blows for practice has not fulfilled his responsibility.

5. And what Mishnah says this?[67] "If a man blew the first *tekiah*[68] [as usual], then prolonged the second so as to make it equal to two, that is reckoned to him only as one blast.[69]

Rabbi Abba bar Z'mina in the name of Rabbi Zeira: even one blast is not reckoned to him. Why? The beginning is joined to the end, and the end is joined to the beginning. The beginning has no end, and the end has no beginning.[70]

Halakhah 4

1. Said Rabbi Jonah: in order that they should *bend* their heart in prayer.[71]

2. They sounded the shofar before Rabbi Joshua ben Levi on the Fast Day.

3. Rabbi Jose asked: and should they not [also] sound the trumpet before him? And he did not recall that which was taught: trumpets in the Temple, no trumpets outside of Jerusalem.[72]

4. And let them pray before him 24![73]

66. The comment is on the end of Mishnah 2, where it says that the shofar is sounded for a long note, and the trumpets are sounded for a short note. Korban Ha'edah points out that the full blast must be heard to fulfill one's responsibility. Hence we must understand the Mishnah to mean that first the trumpets are sounded for a short note, and when they are completely finished the shofar is sounded for a long note.

67. Where is the source of the teaching that one has not fulfilled his obligation until he has heard the entire *tekiah* from beginning to end?

68. Of one set of three, a *tekiah*, a *teruah*, and a second *tekiah*.

69. Mishnah R.H. 4:11.

70. Each individual *tekiah* requires its own distinct beginning and end. In this instance, the final *tekiah* of one set is combined with the first *tekiah* of the next set. But the *tekiah* which constitutes the first half of the blast does not have its own end, the second half its own beginning. Hence "even one blast is not reckoned to him," since it is not a valid blast. The one blast mentioned in Mishnah R.H. 4:11 refers rather to the first *tekiah* in the set.

71. This midrashic comment on Mishnah 3:3 regarding the shofar explains why "on fast days they are from rams, *curved.* . . ." This explanation is based upon a Hebrew word-play.

72. Literally, in the border towns. According to Psalms 98:6, *With trumpets and the sound of the shofar, shout ye* before the King, *the Lord.* Since "before the King" implies in the Temple, the trumpets are not to be sounded outside.

73. In Taanit, chapter 2, it specifies that they add six benedictions to the eighteen regular daily ones in the case of public fasts. This was not limited to the

5. It is like this: Rabbi Yoḥanan prayed twenty-four on the 9th of Av; and he commanded his students not to learn from this case. For it was doubtful to him whether it is a mourning [day],[74] or whether it is a public fast.[75]

6. Rabbi Jose in the name of Rabbi Joshua ben Levi: it is not a public fast.

7. Rabbi Jonah [in the name of] Rabbi Isaac bar Naḥman in the name of Rabbi Joshua ben Levi: it is a mourning [day], it is not a public fast.

8. Rabbi Zeira stated: this view of Rabbi Yoḥanan teaches that the individual prays four on the 9th of Av. Only twenty-four is stated, not four.[76]

Halakhah 5

1. *I am the Lord your God* (Leviticus 23:22)—this indicates the kingship-verses.[77] *A memorial proclaimed with the blast of horns* (Leviticus 23:24)—this indicates the remembrance-verses. *The blast of the horn* (Leviticus 25:9)—this indicates the shofar-verses. Up to here refers to Rosh Hashanah.

2. Jubilee? *Then you shall make proclamation with the blast of the horn on the tenth day in the seventh month, on the Day of Atonement . . .* (Leviticus 25:9). For Scriptures do not have to say "in the seventh month." What do Scriptures mean by "in

---

Temple. Hence they should pray twenty-four benedictions before R. Joshua ben Levi on the Fast Day.

74. And hence would not pray twenty-four benedictions.

75. And hence the twenty-four benedictions were required.

76. I have translated in accordance with the emendation suggested by Rabinovitz, *Sha'are . . .*, p. 278. He understands the passage to mean that when R. Yoḥanan commanded his students above that they not use his praying of twenty-four benedictions on Tishah Be'av as paradigmatic, he was not forbidding them from praying the four prayer services that were obligatory on a public fast-day. Whereas he prayed twenty-four benedictions evening, morning, afternoon, and *ne'ilah*, he did not want the students to follow his example of twenty-four benedictions since, if it is a mourning day, this would not have been appropriate.

77. Lev. 23:22 instructs the people not to reap the corners of their fields nor gather the gleanings of their harvest; rather they are to leave them for the poor and the stranger. Because, the verse concludes, "I am the Lord your God." The implication is that God will judge them if they do not obey. Verses 23 and 24 continue: *And the Lord spoke to Moses, saying, speak to the children of Israel, saying, in the seventh month, on the first day of the month, you shall have a sabbath, a memorial proclaimed with the blast of horns, a holy convocation.* By the hermeneutic principle of juxtaposition, the God of Lev. 23:22, the Lord and King who judges, will do so on the first day of the seventh month.

the seventh month"? Whatever you do on Rosh Hashanah, you
do on the tenth of the month. Just as in the former case there
are kingship-verses, remembrance-verses, and shofar-verses, so
in the latter case there are kingship-verses, remembrance-verses,
and shofar-verses.[78]

3. How do we know scripturally that there is a plain note
before it?[79] Because Scriptures say *Then you shall make proclamation with a shofar [of teruah].*[80] How do we know scripturally
that there is a plain note after it? Because Scriptures say *Then
you shall make proclamation with the shofar.*[81] Up to here refers
to the Jubilee.

4. Rosh Hashanah? *Then you shall make proclamation with
the blast of the horn . . . on the tenth day, on the Day of Atonement* (Leviticus 25:9). For Scriptures do not have to say "in the
seventh month". What do Scriptures mean by "in the seventh
month"? Whatever you do in the seventh month is like on the
tenth of the month. Just as in the former case there is a plain
note and a tremolo and a plain note, so in the latter case there is
a plain note and a tremolo and a plain note.[82]

5. How do we know scripturally that the proper way of blowing the shofar is to sound three sets of three each?[83] Scripture
says *it is a day of* teruah (Numbers 29:1), *a memorial proclaimed with* teruah (Leviticus 23:24), *the* shofar *of* teruah
(Leviticus 25:9). Up to here is like Rabbi Akiba.[84]

78. The operative hermeneutic principle here is the redundant expression.
Since the phrase "in the seventh month" is not essential to identify the day, the
phrase must come to teach us something else that we otherwise would not have
known about the day. Just as Lev. 23:22–24, the verses which serve to establish
the kingship, memorial, and shofar-verses for Rosh Hashanah, contain the
phrase "in the seventh month," so Lev. 25:9, which deals with the Yom Kippur
of the Jubilee year, contains the phrase "in the seventh month," linking them.

79. The text is understanding Lev. 25:9 to read, "then you shall make proclamation with a *shofar* of *teruah*," i.e., the tremulous blast. The question then is,
how does one know scripturally that the *teruah* is preceded by the plain blast, or
tekiah?

80. The word "yha ʿavarta," "then you shall make proclamation," is understood to indicate a *tekiah* blast. "*Teruah*" proves that it is followed with the
tremulous blast.

81. The end of Lev. 25:9. This repetition of the word "ta ʿaviru," "then you
shall make proclamation," indicates a second *tekiah* blast.

82. Lev. 25:9 clearly indicates that the day under consideration is Yom Kippur, the tenth day of the month, and hence the phrase "in the seventh month" is
superfluous. Hence the phrase comes to establish an analogy of expressions with
Lev. 23:24, which deals with Rosh Hashanah. Therefore the order of blasts established above for the Yom Kippur of the Jubilee is applied by analogy to Rosh
Hashanah.

83. Mishnah R.H. 4:9; Tosefta 2:15.

84. Akiba's method of deriving the three sets of three is to take three verses

6. Like Rabbi Ishmael? Rabbi Ishmael taught: *And you shall blow a teruah* (Numbers 10:5), *and you shall blow a teruah a second time* (Numbers 10:6), *they shall blow a teruah for their journeys* (Numbers 10:6).

7. If you would argue that the *tekiah* and the *teruah* are one, is it not written, *but when the assembly is to be gathered together, you shall blow a tekiah, but not a teruah?* (Numbers 10:7).[85]

8. "Jubilee"—even though they did not come under the law of limitation of the Sabbatical year; even though they did not blow the shofar.[86]

9. Or perhaps even though they did not release slaves? Scripture says, *it is a [Jubilee]* (Leviticus 25:10). These are the words of Rabbi Judah.[87]

10. Rabbi Jose said: "Jubilee"—even though they did not come under the law of limitation of the Sabbatical year; even though they did not release slaves.[88]

11. Or perhaps even though they did not blow the shofar? Scripture says, *it is a [Jubilee]* (Leviticus 25:10).[89]

12. Said Rabbi Jose: since Scripture makes it dependent

---

describing Rosh Hashanah which each employ the term "teruah," or tremolo. We have already learned above with regard to the proclamation of the Jubilee that a *tekiah* precedes and follows the *teruah* in each set. We have also learned that the same is true of Rosh Hashanah.

85. In each of R. Ishmael's three proofs, the verb "to blow" is a form of the Hebrew root for *tekiah*. Hence the question being raised is whether the *tekiah* and the *teruah* are both sounded in the same blast. However, Num. 10:7, which immediately follows his three proof-texts, proves that the *tekiah* and the *teruah* constitute separate blasts.

86. The comment is on the precise phrasing of Lev. 25:8–11. Scripture states that one counts forty-nine years, and then one hallows the fiftieth year by sounding the horn loudly in the seventh month, the tenth day of the month, which is the Day of Atonement. Then the text continues: *you shall proclaim liberty throughout the land for all its inhabitants.* The problem is that the next phrase reads: *it shall be a Jubilee for you.* Both Korban Ha'edah and P'ne Moshe comment that in the light of what immediately precedes, *it shall be a Jubilee for you* seems superfluous and hence comes to teach something which we otherwise would not know, that is, it is a Jubilee in any case, even if one did not do the acts specified above. And by virtue of its status as a Jubilee, one does not sow, reap the aftergrowth, or harvest the untrimmed vines.

87. R. Judah warns that one might erroneously likewise consider manumission unessential for the Jubilee. However the statement in Lev. 25:10, "it is a Jubilee," assumes manumission.

88. R. Jose argues that the superfluous phrase "it shall be a Jubilee for you" comes to teach that it is a Jubilee in any case, even if one did not come under the law of limitation of the Sabbatical year or manumit.

89. "It is a Jubilee" assumes the blowing of the shofar to be essential for the Jubilee.

upon the blowing of the shofar,[90] and another verse makes it dependent upon releasing slaves,[91] why do I say that there can be a Jubilee without releasing slaves? Because it is possible that there be a Jubilee without releasing slaves,[92] but it is not possible that there be a Jubilee without blowing of the shofar.

13. Another interpretation: the blowing of the shofar is dependent upon the Court, but the releasing of slaves is dependent upon each individual.[93]

14. And it is in accordance with the opinion of Rabbi Samuel bar Rav Isaac: *and the Lord spoke to Moses and Aaron and gave them a charge unto the children of Israel* (Exodus 6:13). Concerning what did He command them? Concerning the Torah portion on releasing slaves.[94]

15. And it is in accordance with the opinion of Rabbi Ila: Israel was only punished because of the Torah portion on releasing slaves. As Scripture says: *at the end of seven years you shall let go every man his brother that is a Hebrew*, etc. (Jeremiah 34:14).[95]

16. It was taught in the name of Rabbi Nehemiah: *She is like the merchants' ships, and she brings her food from afar* (Proverbs 31:14). The words of Scripture are poor in their place, and rich in another place.[96]

17. Said Rabbi Yoḥanan: These are the words of Rabbi Judah and Rabbi Jose; but according to the Sages, sanctification by the Court, blowing of the shofar, and cancelling of debts cause one to come under the law of limitation of the Sabbatical year.

90. Lev. 25:9.
91. See Lev. 25:40; 25:54–55.
92. Korban Haᵓedah suggests that at a given time Hebrew slaves may not be present in Israel.
93. And the individual could delay and hence nullify the Jubilee, which is the reason why Scripture does not make the Jubilee dependent upon manumission.
94. This serves to prove scripturally that the releasing of slaves is dependent upon each individual. In Jer. 34:12–14, God tells Jeremiah that He *made a covenant with your fathers in the day that I brought them forth out of the land of Egypt, out of the house of bondage, saying: "at the end of seven years you shall let go every man his brother that is a Hebrew, that has been sold to you, and has served you six years, you shall let him go free from you. . . ."* Jeremiah's covenant, according to R. Samuel bar Rav Isaac, is Ex. 6:13.
95. Jer. 34:17 continues with the punishment for noncompliance: *Therefore thus says the Lord: you have not hearkened to Me, to proclaim liberty, every man to his brother, and every man to his neighbor; behold, I proclaim for you a liberty, says the Lord, to the sword, to the pestilence, and to the famine; and I will make you a horror to all the kingdoms of the earth. . . .*
96. Torah is here likened to the "Woman of Valor." The covenantal agreement attributed to Ex. 6:13 is only learned in Jer. 34:17.

18. Granted sanctification by the Court and blowing of the shofar; but regarding cancellation of debts, are they not cancelled at the end?[97]

(59a)   19. Rabbi Zeira learned it from this: *Then he said to me, fear not, Daniel, for from the first day that you set your heart to understand and to chasten yourself before your God your words were heard* (Daniel 10:12)—your words had already been heard.[98]

20. Said Rabbi Yoḥanan: the reasoning of Rabbi Judah is to use the accessible for the frequent and the inaccessible for the infrequent.[99]

Halakhah 6

1. "A shofar which was split and which one stuck back together is invalid."[100] For whom was it necessary [to state]? For Rabbi Nathan.

2. "If one stuck back together pieces of shofars, it is invalid."[101] Also this is for Rabbi Nathan.[102]

3. "If it was perforated and one plugged the hole:"[101] Rabbi

---

97. Deut. 15:1 reads: *at the end of every seven years you shall make a release*. Rabinovitz, *Shaʾare . . .* , p. 278, emends the passage to read as follows: "but according to the Sages, the releasing of slaves, the blowing of the shofar, and the return of landed property to the seller [in the year of the Jubilee] are indispensable. Granted the releasing of slaves and the blowing of the shofar; but regarding the return of landed property to the seller, are they not remitted at the end?" Rabinovitz substitutes the return of property to its original owner for cancellation of debts, because he argues that debts are not cancelled in the Jubilee year. And since the land cannot be worked by the current or prior owner in the Jubilee year, it is returned at the end.

98. Even though the debts might not be cancelled until the end of seven years, their intent to do so could be known a priori.

99. This comment is on R. Judah's ruling at the end of Mishnah R.H. 3:4 that "on the New Year they sound those of rams, and at the Jubilee Year those of wild goats." R. Yoḥanan surmises that the relatively accessible ram's horn is to be used on the relatively frequently occurring New Year, whereas the less accessible horn of the mountain goat is reserved for the very special and rare occasion of the Jubilee, which occurs only once every fifty years.

100. Mishnah Rosh Hashanah 3:5. Korban Haʾedah comments that if it was stuck back together with glue, it is invalid because it is like two shofars, even though throughout its entire length it appears to be but one. The reason that it must be expressly prohibited is because it is not prohibited under the strictures from R. Nathan further on, which ban perforated shofars that have been plugged with a different substance. Even though glue clearly is "a different substance," it would not be visible or recognizable when used to repair a split shofar.

101. Mishnah Rosh Hashanah 3:5.

102. It is necessary to expressly prohibit shofars which have been broken into

Ḥiyya in the name of Rabbi Yoḥanan said that it is the view of
Rabbi Nathan, for it is taught:[103] if it was perforated and one
plugged the hole, whether with the same substance or a different
substance, if [the plugged hole] affects the blowing, it is invalid;
and if not, valid. Rabbi Nathan says: with the same substance,
valid; with a different substance, invalid.[104]

4. Rabbi Ḥiyya in the name of Rabbi Yoḥanan: so is the Mishnah to be read, if it [the perforation] interfered with the blowing
[before it was plugged] it is invalid [after it was plugged]; and if
not, valid.

5. Rabbi Abba bar Z'mina in the name of Rabbi Zeira: [the
above understanding of the Mishnah applies] provided that one
plugged the hole, but if one did not plug it, it is valid, for all of
the sounds are valid on a shofar.

6. Rabbi Jacob bar Aḥa said: Abba bar Abba asked Rabbi,
what is the situation with regard to a pierced shofar? He said to
him: they blew one like that in Yavneh. Rabbi Abba asked before
Rav, what is the situation with regard to a pierced shofar? He
said to him: they blew one like that in Ein Tav.[105]

Halakhah 7[106]

1. Said Rabbi Jose ben Ḥanina: it only said "and so too regarding one who was passing." But if he stood still the assumption is that he paid attention.

---

pieces and stuck back together because they also would not be prohibited under
the strictures from R. Nathan which follow.

103. Tosefta Rosh Hashanah 2:4.

104. Mishnah 3:5 deals with three cases: (1) a shofar which was split and
stuck back together; (2) a shofar broken into pieces and stuck back together; (3) a
shofar which was perforated and plugged. According to the Rabbis, even a
plugged perforation which affects the sound is invalid. From this it goes without
saying that a more serious impediment to the sound, i.e., a split or a complete
break into pieces, would render the shofar invalid. Hence cases (1) and (2) can
be derived by an inference a fortiori from (3) if one follows the Rabbis, and
hence these two cases need not be stated. Yet they were stated, and the implicit
question is, why? The answer is, to set off cases (1) and (2) from case (3) as
decided by R. Nathan.

105. In the Babylonian Talmud R.H. 27b, the text comments that "All shofars
are pierced!" since by definition a shofar is a horn that has been pierced. R. Ashi
clarifies by explaining that what is meant is a shofar with a pierced inset bone,
i.e., the bony projection from the animal's head over which the horny substance
grows. Usually the inset bone is extracted to produce a shofar, but here it is not
removed but merely pierced. Such a shofar was apparently acceptable for use on
Rosh Hashanah in two different seats of the Court.

106. On Mishnah 3:6.

2. If one placed one shofar within another and blew, if one heard the sound of the inner one, he has fulfilled his obligation, if one heard the sound of the outer one, he has not fulfilled his obligation.[107]

3. Rabbi Abbina asked: what is the situation if one reversed it? We learn from this: if one shaved it down, whether inside or outside, it is valid. It only said "shaved it down." But if one reversed it, it is invalid. What is the relationship of the one to the other? That negates its cavity, and that does not negate its cavity.[108]

Halakhah 8

1. Rabbi Joshua ben Levi said: Amalek was a believer in sorcery. What did he do? He would cause men to come forth [for battle] on their birthdays, thinking that a man would not fall readily on his birthday.

2. What did Moses do? He confounded the order of the planets. As it is written: *The sun and the moon stood still in their habitation*, etc. (Habbakuk 3:11). And it is written: *the deep uttered his voice, and lifted up his hands on high* (Habbakuk 3:10). From on high he[109] lifted his hands, the deep uttered his[110] voice.

3. Samuel cited the verse: *The host will be set [upon Israel] because of transgression against that which is [to be studied] continually* (Daniel 8:12)—that is, transgression against the Torah. *And it cast truth to the ground.* When Israel cast words of Torah to the ground, this evil kingdom enacts decrees and succeeds.

4. What is the proof? *And it cast truth to the ground; and it practiced and prospered* (Daniel 8:12). "And truth" means only

107. Tosefta 2:4.
108. According to P'ne Moshe, "reversing it" means switching the ends so as to make the narrow end the bell and the bell end the mouthpiece. Although, following the Tosefta Rosh Hashanah 2:4 reading, "if one shaved it down, whether inside or outside, it is valid," the reversed shofar would nonetheless be invalid because in addition to considerable scraping and reshaping, it would also "negate its [original] cavity." The P.T. reading which has been replaced by the Tosefta is: if one shaved it down inside, it is invalid; outside, valid.
    Korban Ha'edah understands R. Abbina's question differently. "What is the situation if one turned it inside out?" He likens it to the turning inside out of a garment, probably after softening it with hot water.
109. Moses.
110. According to P'ne Moshe, Israel triumphed over Amalek, who descended until *the deep uttered his voice.*

Torah. As it is written: *Buy the truth and sell it not, wisdom
and instruction and understanding* (Proverbs 23:23).

5. Said Rabbi Judah bar Pazzi: *Israel has cast off that which
is good, the enemy will pursue him* (Hosea 8:3). And "good"
means only Torah. As it is written: *For a good doctrine have I
given unto you, my Torah, do not forsake it* (Proverbs 4:2).

Halakhah 9

1. Said Rabbi Jose: in four places "make for yourself" is
said. In three it is explained, and in one it is not. *Make for
yourself an ark of gopher wood* (Genesis 6:14), *make for yourself two silver trumpets* (Numbers 10:2), *make for yourself
knives of flint* (Joshua 5:2), but *make for yourself a fiery serpent* (Numbers 21:8) is not explained.[111]

2. Said Moses: is not its[112] real name *naḥash*? Therefore *And
Moses made a brass [neḥoshet] serpent [naḥash]*.

3. Like this case Rabbi Meir used to expound names. The
name of one man was Kidor. Rabbi Meir said to them: hide
yourself from him; he is a wicked man *for a generation [ki-dor]
very froward are they* (Deuteronomy 32:20).

4. Rabbi Levi in the name of Rabbi Ḥama bar Ḥanina: "and
it shall come to pass that one who is bitten" is not written here;
rather . . . *everyone who is bitten* (Numbers 21:8), whether the
bite of a dog or a snake.[113]

But they are not alike. With regard to the bite of a dog Scripture says *[everyone who is bitten,] when he sees [it, shall live]*;
with regard to the bite of a snake Scripture says *[if a serpent had
bitten any man,] when he beheld [the serpent of brass, he lived]*
(Numbers 21:9).[114]

5. Rabbi Judah Gozrayah[115] in the name of Rabbi Aḥa: with
regard to the bite of a dog, which is not of its species, Scripture
says *when he sees*; with regard to the bite of a snake, which is of
its species, Scripture says *when he beheld*.[116]

---

111. The text does not specify of what material the serpent was to be made.
112. The fiery serpent's.
113. P'ne Moshe suggests that the use of the word *kol* (everyone) serves as
an extension to include those bitten by beasts other than the snake. Korban
Ha'edah says that the text should read: "even the bite of a dog, an asp, a scor-
pion, or a wild animal," drawing upon the parallel text in Numbers Rabbah
19:23. Hence *everyone* who had been bitten and sees the fiery serpent shall live.
114. The implication is that the cure from snakebite requires a more intense
and focused kind of look.
115. Perhaps R. Judah the circumciser or R. Judah of Gezer.
116. Since a dog is not of the same species as the brass serpent, a glance at the

6. And the Rabbis said: with regard to the bite of a dog, which does not penetrate, Scripture says *when he sees*; with regard to the bite of a snake, which does penetrate, *when he beheld.*[117]

Halakhah 10

1. It is taught:[118] but they said,[119] a woman may recite Grace for her husband,[120] a slave for his master, a minor for his father.

2. Granted that a woman may recite Grace for her husband, a slave for his master, but a minor for his father?

3. Did not Rabbi Aḥa in the name of Rabbi Jose the son of Rabbi N'horai say thusly: all that they said with regard to the minor was merely intended in order to initiate him [into religious practices].[121]

The difficulty may be solved by repeating after them.[122] It is like that which we have been taught there:[123] "If a slave, a woman, or a minor recited [the Hallel] to him, he must repeat after them what they say (and let it be a curse unto him)."[124] [And they said further]:[125] Let a curse come upon a man of twenty who is dependent upon a boy of ten.

snake suffices to effect healing. A snake and the brass serpent represent the same species; therefore the victim must take a more careful look and must pay close attention.

117. Because the venom of the snake quickly penetrates the body of the victim, he must take a more intense look.

118. Tosefta Berachot 5 : 17. Parallels are Berachot, chapter 3, Halakhah 3, and Sukah, chapter 3, Halakhah 9.

119. The Tosefta passage reads, "*in fact* they said." According to B.T. Baba Metsia 60a, "wherever an opinion is introduced with the words 'in fact they said,' it means to say that it is an established legal rule."

120. And therefore effectively act on his behalf, exempting him.

121. The minor does not exempt the father by reciting the blessing after meals. Rather the Rabbis permitted him so that he might become accustomed to practicing religious precepts.

122. The manuscript of R.H. plus all the manuscript parallels read: "The difficulty may be solved by repeating after them *Amen*." The word "Amen" is missing in the printed text of Rosh Hashanah, and the elimination appears correct in the light of Mishnah Sukah 3 : 10.

123. Mishnah Sukah 3 : 10.

124. The implication is that the man is ignorant and hence unable to fulfill his obligation to say the Hallel, so he exempts himself by reciting word for word after a slave, woman, or minor.

125. The words in brackets appear as an addition in another hand in the margin of the Sukah parallel in the Leiden MS. They appear in the text proper in the Berachot parallel in the Serilio MS. They do not appear in the Leiden R.H. In the Leiden and Vatican Berachot parallels it reads: "but they said," a repeat of the words we find at the beginning of Halakhah 10.

4 Mishnah Rosh Hashanah
Chapter Four

1. When the Holiday of the New Year fell on a Sabbath, they used to sound the shofar in the Temple, but not in the provinces.[1] After the Temple was destroyed, Rabbi Yoḥanan ben Zakkai decreed that they should sound the shofar wherever there was a Court. Rabbi Eleazar said: Rabban Yoḥanan ben Zakkai only decreed that they should sound the shofar in Yavneh. They said to him: there is no difference whether it is Yavneh or any other place where there is a Court.[2]

2. And in this regard also was Jerusalem ahead of Yavneh:[3] in every town which is within sight[4] and range of sound,[5] near,[6] and [with folk] able to come [up to Jerusalem],[7] they sound the

---

1. Albeck, in his Mishnah, follows the Rambam in interpreting "in the Temple" to mean "in the place of the Temple," i.e. all of Jerusalem. He understands "in the provinces" to mean all other towns. Pʾne Moshe follows the Rambam, whereas Korban Haʾedah understands "in the provinces" to include Jerusalem outside of the Temple precincts. The concern is not the sounding of the shofar per se, but rather that one might unintentionally carry it "in the provinces."

2. The assumption is that the presence of a Court assures the scrupulous adherence to the laws which pertain to the Sabbath.

3. With regard to the sounding of the shofar on the Sabbath. The B.T. 30a asks why the Mishnah reads "and in this regard *also*," since a first superiority is not stated explicitly in the Mishnah. The answer given there is that in Jerusalem they blew whether or not they were in the presence of the Court, but in Yavneh, they only blew before the Court.

4. This would exclude from the category of places where the shofar could be sounded on the Sabbath a low-lying town whose inhabitants could not see Jerusalem.

5. This would exclude a town which sits up high on a hill or has a hill between it and Jerusalem.

6. This would exclude a town beyond the Sabbath limit.

7. This would exclude a town sufficiently close to Jerusalem, but cut off from access by some obstacle, such as water.

shofar. But as to Yavneh, they sound the shofar only in the Court alone.

3. Originally the *lulav* was carried in the Temple for seven days,[8] and in the provinces one day. After the Temple was destroyed, Rabban Yoḥanan ben Zakkai decreed that the *lulav* be carried in the provinces for seven days as a remembrance of the Temple; and [he decreed] that on the entire Day of Waving it be forbidden [to eat of new produce].[9]

4. Originally they used to accept testimony with regard to the New Moon[10] all the day.[11] Once the witnesses delayed so long in coming that they disrupted the Levites in their singing;[12] therefore they decreed that they should not accept [witnesses] beyond the *Minḥah* period. And if people came after *Minḥah*, they observed that day and the next as holy.[13] After the Temple was destroyed, Rabban Yoḥanan ben Zakkai decreed that they should accept testimony with regard to the New Moon all the day.[14]

5. Rabbi Joshua ben Korḥah said: and Rabban Yoḥanan ben

8. The scriptural basis is Lev. 23:40–41.

9. The scriptural commandment and requirements for the Day of Waving are found in Lev. 23:9–14. See also Mishnah Sukah 3:12–14.

The day of the waving of the *Omer*, the day after Passover (the sixteenth of Nisan), the new grain was taken to the Temple, and after the sheaf was waved and the appropriate offerings were made, they could eat of the new produce. Rabban Yoḥanan ben Zakkai forbid consumption of the new produce until the seventeenth of Nisan.

10. Of the New Year in Tishri.

11. The entire thirtieth of Elul. From the beginning of the thirtieth they observed it as a holiday, because at any moment witnesses to the New Moon might arrive to testify, making this the New Moon and New Year's day.

12. Num. 28:4 specifies that the daily *Tamid* offering be morning and afternoon. Mishnah Pesachim 5:1 adds that the daily evening burnt offering was slaughtered at 2:30 P.M. and offered up at 3:30 P.M. On the New Moon Day, Additional Offerings specified in Num. 28:11–14 followed the Tamid. The Levites had to know before the *Tamid* whether this day was to be the thirtieth of Elul or *Rosh Ḥodesh* Tishri, because they needed to know whether to accompany the Daily Whole Offering with the singing of the ordinary weekday Psalm or the Holiday Psalm (see Mishnah Tamid 7:3–4), and whether to include the Additional Offerings. Since the witnesses were late, they delayed the offerings so as to clarify these questions.

13. Once the afternoon Daily Whole Offering had begun, witnesses were made inadmissible, that day was counted as the thirtieth of Elul, and the following day was made *Rosh Ḥodesh* Tishri. Since sundown on the night following the twenty-ninth of Elul they had observed this day as holy in case witnesses arrived before *Minḥah*. Now, even though the witnesses were no longer admissible, they continued to observe the rest of the thirtieth of Elul as well as the first of Tishri as holy.

14. The questions as to the proper Psalm and the Additional Offerings were no longer applicable.

Zakkai also decreed that wherever the head of the Court might
be, the witnesses were to go only to the meeting place.

6. The order of the Benedictions [for the Rosh Hashanah
Musaf]: one says "the Patriarchs," "the Powers," and "the Sanctification of God's Name," and includes with them the Sovereignty Verses, and does not sound the shofar; "Sanctification of
the Day," and sounds the shofar; Remembrance Verses, and
sounds the shofar; Shofar Verses, and sounds the shofar; then one
says "the Temple Service," "the Thanksgiving," and "the Priestly
Benediction"; this is the opinion of Rabbi Yoḥanan ben Nuri.

7. Rabbi Akiba said to him: if one does not sound the shofar
for the Sovereignty Verses, why mention them? Rather one says
"the Patriarchs," "the Powers," and "the Sanctification of God's
Name," and includes the Sovereignty Verses with "the Sanctification of the Day," and sounds the shofar; Remembrance Verses,
and sounds the shofar; Shofar Verses, and sounds the shofar;
then one says "the Temple Service," "the Thanksgiving," and
"the Priestly Benediction."

(59b)   8. They may not recite less than ten Sovereignty Verses, ten
Remembrance Verses, ten Shofar Verses. Rabbi Yoḥanan ben
Nuri said: if one recited three of each, he has fulfilled his obligation. They may not mention Sovereignty, Remembrance, or Shofar Verses which deal with divine retribution. One begins with
verses from the Pentateuch and finishes with verses from the
Prophets. Rabbi Jose says: if one finishes with verses from
the Pentateuch, he has fulfilled his obligation.

9. With regard to the one who passes before the ark [to lead
services] on the Holiday of the New Year, the second reader[15]
orders the blowing of the shofar; but at times when the Hallel
is recited,[16] the first reader recites the Hallel.[17]

10. For the sake of the shofar of the New Year, one does not
transgress the Sabbath limit, or remove because of it a pile of
stones, or climb a tree, or ride on the back of an animal, or swim
on the water; and one may not cut it either with an implement
the use of which is [prohibited] because of the law of Sabbath
rest or an implement the use of which is [prohibited] because of
an explicit biblical prohibition. But if one wants to put wine or
water in it, he may do so. They should not prevent children
from sounding the shofar, rather they should practice with them

15. The reader charged with responsibility for the Additional Service.
16. That is, on the three Pilgrimmage Festivals.
17. Psalms 113–18.

until they learn; but one who is engaged in practice has not fulfilled his obligation, and one who hears another practicing has not fulfilled his obligation.

11. The manner of shofar soundings is three series of three blasts each. The length of the sustained note is the equivalent of three quivering notes. The length of the quivering note is the equivalent of three disconnected short notes.

If first one sounds a sustained blast, and then sustains the second to the equivalent of two, it is accounted to him as one blast only.

Regarding one who had recited the Benedictions, after which a shofar had been assigned to him, he blows a sustained, a quivering, and a sustained blast, a sustained, a quivering, and a sustained blast three times.

Just as the reader of the congregation is obligated [to say the daily *Tefillah*], so likewise is each individual. Rabban Gamaliel says: the reader of the congregation absolves the public of their obligation.

Halakhah 1

Gemara. 1. When the Holiday of the New Year, etc. Rabbi Abba bar Pappa said: Rabbi Yoḥanan and Rabbi Simon ben Lakish were once sitting and puzzling. They said, we are taught in the Mishnah: "when the Holiday of the New Year fell on a Sabbath, they used to sound the shofar in the Temple, but not in the provinces." If it [sounding the shofar] is according to the biblical law, it should supersede [the observance of] the Sabbath in the provinces also, if it is not according to the biblical law, it should not supersede [the observance of] the Sabbath even in the Temple?

2. Kahana passed by. They said: behold a great man. Let us ask him. They went and asked him. He said to them: one scriptural verse says, *it is a day of sounding the shofar* (Numbers 29:1), and one scriptural verse says, *a memorial of the sounding of the shofar* (Leviticus 23:24). How can this be? When it [Rosh Hashanah] happens to fall on a weekday, *it is a day of sounding the shofar*; when it happens to fall on the Sabbath, *a memorial of the sounding of the shofar*—we recall to memory the act of blowing, but we do not actually sound the shofar.

3. Rabbi Zeira urged his colleagues: go in and listen to the voice of Rabbi Levi expounding, for it is impossible that he

would end his weekly scriptural lesson without some instructive observation.

4. He [Rabbi Levi] entered and said before them: one scriptural verse says, *it is a day of sounding the shofar*, and another scriptural verse says, *a memorial of the sounding of the shofar*. How can this be? When it [Rosh Hashanah] happens to fall on a weekday, *it is a day of sounding the shofar*, but when it happens to fall on the Sabbath, *a memorial of the sounding of the shofar*— we recall to memory the act of blowing, but we do not actually sound the shofar.

5. If this were so, then [the sounding of the shofar] even in the Temple should not supersede [the observance of the Sabbath]? It teaches *[and in the seventh month,] on the first day of the month, [you shall have a holy convocation; you shall do no servile work; it is a day of sounding the shofar]* (Numbers 29:1).[18]

6. If this were so, then wherever they know that it is the first day of the month it [the sounding of the shofar] should supersede the Sabbath?[19] Rabbi Simon ben Yoḥai taught: *it is a day of sounding the shofar unto you . . . where you make a burnt offering* (Numbers 29:1–2)[20]—which means in [the Temple], that place where the offerings were brought.

7. The colleagues said before Rabbi Jonah: But is it not written scripturally, *then you shall cause the shofar of the Jubilee to sound in the seventh month [on the tenth day of the month; on the day of Atonement you shall make the shofar sound throughout your land]?* (Leviticus 25:9).[21] He said to them: this you cause to sound throughout your land, but none other.[22]

18. This scriptural verse applies to the Temple, because it was there that they established the New Moon and hence knew when "on the first day of the month" would be.

19. Mishnah R.H. 1:3 tells us that during Temple times messengers went forth in Tishri to proclaim the time of the appearance of the New Moon, and Mishnah 1:4 adds that for the New Moon of Tishri messengers might even profane the Sabbath in going forth to Syria. Clearly messengers might reach well beyond Jerusalem on that day, and would surely notify towns not already permitted to sound the shofar by virtue of the fact that they fit one or more of the categories in Mishnah 4:2.

20. I have followed the readings of the parallel texts in Lev. Rab. 29:12, Pesikta de Rav Kahana 23:12, Yalkut Shimoni Parashat Emor 645, and Pinhas 782 in replacing Lev. 23:25 with Num. 29:1–2 as the proof-text. Since Lev. 23:24 has been interpreted above to mean that on the Sabbath we recall to memory the act of blowing but we do not actually sound the shofar, P.T.'s use of 23:25 (*but you shall make an offering*) does not make sense.

21. The question they are asking R. Jonah is why the shofar of the Jubilee on Yom Kippur should be treated differently from the shofar of the New Year on the Sabbath.

22. I.e., not the shofar of the New Year on the Sabbath.

8. They said to him: or perhaps it means, this you cause to sound throughout your land, but the other both in and outside the land. Said Rabbi Jonah: if it were written scripturally, "you shall cause the shofar to sound throughout your land," I would say that here is a limitation and in the other place an expansion;[23] but since it says "throughout *all* of your land," here is an expansion and in the other place a limitation.[24]

Halakhah 2

1. Provided that all of these features [enumerated in the Mishnah] are in it. [This excludes every town] which is within sight but not range of sound, for example where Jerusalem is above and a town below; or within range of sound but not sight, because a hill intervenes; or within sight and range of sound but [with folk] not able to come [up to Jerusalem] because they are outside of the Sabbath limit; or within sight and range of sound and sufficiently close but [with folk] not able to come [up to Jerusalem] because a river intervenes.

2. Rabbi Jonah asked: [what if the town has folk] able to come [to Jerusalem] by means of establishing ʾeruvim?[25]

3. As you say concerning Jerusalem that in every town which is within sight and range of sound, near, and [with folk] able to come [up to Jerusalem], they sound the shofar;[26] say thus with regard to Yavneh! Jerusalem is scripturally prescribed, and the towns near it are scripturally prescribed;[27] whereas Yavneh is a

---

23. Understanding Lev. 25:9 to mean "you shall cause the shofar to sound *only* throughout your land," which differentiates it from the shofar of the New Year on the Sabbath, which is to be sounded everywhere.

24. The fact that Lev. 25:9 says "throughout *all* of your land" serves to differentiate it from the shofar of the New Year on the Sabbath, which is only sounded in part of the land—in the Temple.

25. According to the Mishnah, the town must be "near," that is, within the Sabbath limit, so that its residents could come up to Jerusalem. R. Jonah wants to know if these requirements are met if one uses the rabbinic legal fiction of an ʾeruv to transfer his Sabbath abode to the Sabbath limit so that movements on the Sabbath could then be measured with this new location as the center. Note that the question remains unanswered.

26. This statement from the Mishnah is a rabbinical ordinance expanding the biblical command to blow the shofar on Rosh Hashanah which is found in Num. 29:1–2. As we saw above, the Rabbis learned from Num. 29:2 that the shofar should be sounded in the Temple (Jerusalem) on the Sabbath, and this includes the towns immediately contingent to Jerusalem.

27. The text continues as follows: "and Rabban Yoḥanan ben Zakkai introduced a measure extending a biblical law." I have followed the emendation suggested by Rabinovitz, Shaʾare . . . , p. 279 in eliminating this sentence as an

rabbinical ordinance, and the towns near it are rabbinical ordinance, and can Rabban Yoḥanan ben Zakkai introduce a measure
extending a rabbinical ordinance? Is there rabbinical ordinance
upon rabbinical ordinance?[28]

4. Rabbi Simon in the name of Rabbi Joshua ben Levi: when
the Court left its [normal] location for another, they did not sound
the shofar.[29]

5. Rabbi Jose asked before Rabbi Simon: even from house to
house, even from the reception room to the sleeping room? He
said to him: my master,[30] I learned up to here.[31]

Halakhah 3

1. It is written: *and you shall rejoice before the Lord your
God seven days* (Leviticus 23:40).

Some authorities teach: Scripture is speaking about the rejoicing of Peace Offerings.

Other authorities teach: Scripture is speaking about the rejoicing of *lulav.*

Following the one who said that Scripture is speaking about
the rejoicing of *lulav,*[32] the first day is scripturally prescribed,[33]
and the remaining days are scripturally prescribed,[34] and Rabban
Yoḥanan ben Zakkai introduced a measure extending a biblical law.

Following the one who said that Scripture is speaking about
the rejoicing of Peace Offerings,[35] the first day is scripturally prescribed[33] and the remaining days are rabbinically prescribed,[36]

incorrect expansion of this text based upon a similar structural pattern further on
in Halakhah 3, paragraph 1, which contains the same sentence.

28. Can Mishnah 4:2, "in every town which is . . . ," be applied as well to
Yavneh as to Jerusalem? The obvious answer is "no, there is no rabbinical ordinance upon rabbinical ordinance."

29. According to the Mishnah, in Yavneh they can sound the shofar only in
the Court alone, that is, only in the actual presence of the Court.

30. R. Jose was addressed this way out of courtesy. I have followed the emendation suggested by Rabinovitz, *Shaʾare . . . ,* p. 279. The text reads: "in the
school of my master. . . ."

31. That is, these are the words I heard. No more.

32. The manuscripts and the printed texts read "the rejoicing of Peace Offerings," but these texts have incorrectly reversed the order.

33. *And you shall take for yourselves on the first day* . . . (Lev. 23:40). This
proves that on the first day one "rejoices" even in the provinces.

34. "And you shall rejoice *before the Lord your God* seven days" (Lev.
23:40). This proves that the *lulav* was carried in the Temple for seven days.

35. The manuscripts and the printed texts read "the rejoicing of *lulav,*" but
these texts have incorrectly reversed the order. See footnote 32 above.

36. And you shall rejoice *before the Lord your God* seven days" (Lev. 23:40)

and Rabban Yoḥanan ben Zakkai introduced a measure extending a rabbinical ordinance? Is there rabbinical ordinance upon
rabbinical ordinance?

2. The colleagues asked Rabbi Jonah: it is written there: *and
you shall offer an offering made by fire unto the Lord seven days*
(Leviticus 23 : 8)—there is no seven exclusive of the Sabbath.[37]
And like it, and *you shall rejoice before the Lord your God
seven days* (Leviticus 23 : 40)—there is no seven exclusive of the
Sabbath?[38]

He said to them: it is different, for it is written, *and you shall
take for yourselves on the first day* (Leviticus 23 : 40)—the first
is separated off from them.[39]

3. In that case, in the Temple it should supersede [the Sab-
bath], but in the provinces it should not supersede?[40]

Said Rabbi Jonah: if it were written scripturally, "and you
shall take . . . *before the Lord your God*," I would have said
that here is a limitation[41] and in the other place an extension;[42]
but [since it says] "and you shall take *for yourselves*,"[43] [this
means] in any place;[44] "and you shall rejoice *before the Lord
your God* seven days," [this means] in Jerusalem.

---

refers to the rejoicing of Peace Offerings in the Temple, and hence not to *lulav*.
Therefore seven days of *lulav* in the Temple are rabbinically prescribed, and
Rabban Yoḥanan's decree extending the seven days of *lulav* to the provinces
would be a rabbinical ordinance upon rabbinical ordinance. Since this is not
possible, we know that Lev. 23 : 40 must refer to *lulav*.

37. And hence this verse serves to prove that this Passover offering supersedes
the Sabbath.

38. Lev. 23 : 40 seems to say that the rejoicing of *lulav* in the Temple also
continues for seven days and supersedes the Sabbath. Yet then Mishnah Sukah
4 : 2, which says that *lulav* supersedes only if the first day of the festival falls on
the Sabbath, makes no sense.

39. And since *lulav* on the first day is treated separately in Scriptures, it alone
supersedes when it falls on the Sabbath.

40. If the instructions in Lev. 23 : 40a serve to set off day one from the rest of
the seven days of rejoicing in the Temple (before the Lord your God—23 : 40b),
they distinguish it only with regard to superseding Sabbath in the Temple and
say nothing about the provinces.

41. *Lulav* when day 1 falls on the Sabbath supersedes only in the Temple. The
R.H. text reads "an extension," but I have followed the parallel text from Sukah
3, Hal. 13.

42. Observe *lulav* in the provinces for one day which is not the Sabbath. The
R.H. text reads "a limitation," but I have followed the parallel text from Sukah
3, Hal. 13.

43. Without the limitation "before the Lord your God."

44. Lev. 23 : 40a serves to set off day 1 with regard to superseding the Sabbath
anywhere.

Halakhah 4

1. Said Rabbi Samuel bar Naḥman: because of an event that took place.[45] Once an alarm spread in town, and the Saracens came and took them, and the Levites became disordered in their singing.[46]

2. Said Rabbi Aḥa bar Pappa before Rabbi Zeira: the colleagues asked before Rabbi Samuel bar Naḥman, in the name of whom did Rabbi say it? He said to them, "am I like you who have many teachers? I said it in the name of Rabbi Joshua ben Levi."

3. And Rabbi Ila[47] brings this basis of the *halakhah*.[48] For it is taught in a *baraita*: "on the fifth day they sang, *sing aloud unto God our strength* (Psalms 81:2); and on Rosh Hashanah they

(59c)   sang *I removed his shoulder from the burden* (Psalms 81:7).[49]

4. If the Holiday fell on the fifth day, in the morning they sang *sing aloud unto God our strength*,[50] and in the afternoon they sang *I removed his shoulder from the burden*.[51] If they came before *Minḥah*, they sang *I removed his shoulder from the burden*.[52] If they came after *Minḥah*, they sang *sing aloud unto God our strength*.[53] But does this not result in singing a song and then repeating it?[54]

5. Rabbi Ada of Caesarea in the name of Rabbi Yoḥanan: most of the day had already passed in holiness.[55]

45. He is explaining the delay of the witnesses mentioned in the Mishnah which led the Levites to become disordered in their afternoon Psalm.

46. Korban Ha²edah understands this abbreviated version of the story to mean that once a rumor spread through town that Saracen robbers had come and seized the witnesses who had come to testify concerning the appearance of the New Moon. This caused the Levites to become disordered in their singing, since they thought that the witnesses might still be released in time for their testimony to be heard, the day sanctified, and the Holiday Psalm sung. Hence they refrained from singing anything.

47. The text reads: "and Rabbi doesn't bring the basis of the *halakhah*." However I have followed the emendation suggested by Korban Ha²edah, reading "*lo*" as Ila.

48. That is, the reason for the disorder among the Levites can be found in the *baraita* which follows.

49. According to P²ne Moshe, on Rosh Hashanah they began Psalm 81 with verse 7 because on that day Joseph went out from the prison.

50. The normal Thursday Psalm, since witnesses would rarely have arrived before the morning offering.

51. Since witnesses generally would have arrived before *Minḥah*.

52. The Leiden MS reads *sing aloud unto God our strength*, but this is wrong.

53. Someone who edited the Leiden MS for the printed versions has scratched out this sentence. However, it belongs here, although it is missing from the printed texts.

54. Hence this is the disarrangement which occurred in the Levites' singing.

55. An explanation for the mishnaic assertion that if the witnesses came after

6. Said Rabbi Ḥiyyah bar Abba: R. Yoḥanan commanded those of the synagogue of Kufra[56] to be careful[57] to take [the food for the feast of intercalation] and to come in while it is yet daytime, and they came reciting "its due time and its intercalated time."[58]

Halakhah 5

1. So is the Mishnah to be read: to the meeting place for declaring the New Moon.[59]

Halakhah 6

1. In Judah they followed the custom of Rabbi Akiba, and in the Galilee that of Rabbi Yoḥanan ben Nuri. If one transgressed and did in Judah like the Galilee,[60] or in the Galilee like Judah,[61] he has fulfilled his responsibilities.

Now when they sanctified the year in Usha, on the first day Rabbi Ishmael the son of Rabbi Yoḥanan ben Beroqah passed

---

Minḥah, they observed that day and the next as holy. Since the entire day up until *Minḥah* had been observed as a Holiday in case the witnesses should come, they should not change posture now and treat the remainder of the day lightly.

56. A synagogue in Tiberias, the place where R. Yoḥanan established his academy.

57. I am following the emendation suggested by Rabinovitz, *Shaʾare . . .* , p. 279, in reading *skhin*. See Jastrow, p. 989, under *skhy*.

58. A highly problematic passage. I have based my translation upon interpretations suggested by Rabinovitz, *Shaʾare . . .* , pp. 279 and 296, and Lieberman in Tarbiz V, p. 102. Both suggest that the reference is to the feast of intercalation of the month mentioned in Mishnah Sanhedrin 8 : 2 and B.T. 70b. In the B.T. there we learn that this feast was over wheat bread and beans, and took place on the evening following the intercalated day.

Lieberman says R. Yoḥanan believed the Torah (1 Sam. 20 : 24–27) prescribes a two-day observance of *Rosh Ḥodesh*. Although the main part of the feast took place in the evening of days 29 and 30, they began while it was still day (i.e., before sunset) so that they could recite "its due time and its intercalated time" as part of a blessing over the wine. Rabinovitz emends the text to read "and they came *feasting* in its due time and its intercalated time."

59. With regard to testifying concerning the New Moon, the prospective witnesses were to go to that place where the Court met, whether the head of the Court was there or not. Even though we learned in chapter 2 : 7 above that it was the head of the Court who announced "it is sanctified," this Mishnah informs us that the witnesses need not pursue him to testify before him. The Court could examine them in his absence.

60. Including the Sovereignty Verses with "the Sanctification of God's Name" and not sounding the shofar.

61. Including the Sovereignty Verses with "the Sanctification of the Day" and sounding the shofar.

106   Chapter Four

[before the ark] and said it in accord with the view of Rabbi Yoḥanan ben Nuri. Said Rabban Simon ben Gamaliel: "that was not the custom which we followed in Yavneh." [62] So on the second day Rabbi Ḥananiah, son of Rabbi Jose the Galilean, passed [before the ark] and said it in accord with the view of Rabbi Yoḥanan ben Nuri. Said Rabban Simon ben Gamaliel: "That was that was the custom which we followed in Yavneh." [63]

2. Rabbi Abbahu said in the name of Rabbi Eleazar: in every instance where one transgressed and mentioned "The Mighty One of Rulership," he has not fulfilled his obligation except for "The Holy God" of the New Year, and that only in the Additional Service. [64] And this is like the opinion of Rabbi Yoḥanan ben Nuri.

3. Rabban Simon ben Gamaliel says: one says "the Sanctification of the Day" with the Remembrance Verses. And this is like the opinion of Rabbi Akiba. [65]

4. Said Rabban Simon ben Gamaliel: just as we find that in every case one says it in the middle, so likewise here one should say it in the middle. [66]

62. The reference is to Simon, son of Gamaliel II. Simon opened an academy in Yavneh and became the Nasi there. Later, he had to transfer his academy, and also the seat of the new Sanhedrin, to Usha, a town in the Galilee.
Simon is indicating that when Gamaliel II was Nasi in Yavneh, they did not follow the practice endorsed by R. Yoḥanan ben Nuri. Although he is now at the head of a Galilean academy, and hence R. Ishmael did the expected in following the view of R. Yoḥanan, Simon makes a point of telling him that this was not the way they used to do it in Yavneh.
63. R. Hanina "did in the Galilee like Judah," and not only fulfilled his responsibilities but also received an active endorsement from Rabban Simon.
64. The third benediction of the daily ʾAmidah, "the Sanctification of the Name," ends "Blessed art Thou, O Lord, the Holy God." One cannot substitute the final phrase "The Mighty One of Rulership" except in the Rosh Hashanah Musaf Service. To do so there would be in concert with the view of R. Yoḥanan, since he said that one includes the Sovereignty Verses with "the Sanctification of God's Name." Therefore to seal the benediction with a phrase indicating God's Sovereignty instead of God's Holiness would be acceptable.
65. He agrees with R. Akiba that the Sovereignty Verses should not be included with "the Sanctification of God's Name." And although R. Akiba includes the Sovereignty Verses with "the Sanctification of the Day" whereas he includes the Remembrance Verses, both result in "the Sanctification of the Day" being followed by the sounding of the shofar.
66. On those days when seven benedictions are said, i.e. the Sabbath and the Three Festivals, "the Sanctification of the Day" is preceded by three benedictions ("the Patriarchs," "the Powers," and "the Sanctification of God's Name") and followed by three ("the Temple Service," "the Thanksgiving," and "the Priestly Benediction"). So likewise on Rosh Hashanah when nine benedictions are said, "the Sanctification of the Day" is in the middle, or fifth. This would preclude the methods of R. Yoḥanan and R. Akiba, since both place "Sanctification of the Day" fourth.

5. Rabbi says: just as we find that in every case one says it fourth, so likewise here one should say it fourth.[67]

6. Rabbi Jacob bar Aḥa [in the name of] Rabbi Zeira [in the name of] Rav Ḥanin bar Abba in the name of Rav: one must say "the Holy God."[68]

7. Rabbi Abba in the name of Abba bar Rav Huna said: one must say "the Holy God, Who does abundantly forgive."[69]

8. Rabbi Abba in the name of Abba bar Jeremiah: in the [daily] ʾAmidah one says "God of David and Builder of Jerusalem;"[70] in the Haftarah benediction one says "the God of David, Who causes salvation to spring forth."[71]

9. "When the Holiday of the New Year fell on a Sabbath"— some authorities teach: one begins with the holiday [formula], and seals with the Sabbath [formula];[72] other authorities teach: one begins with the Sabbath [formula], and seals with the holiday [formula].[73] Rabbi says: one begins with the Sabbath [formula], and seals with the Sabbath [formula], placing the holiday between them.[74] Rabbi Judah bar Pazzi said in the name of Rabbi Joshua ben Levi: the law is according to Rabbi.

67. Since "the Sanctification of the Day" is the fourth benediction on Sabbath and Festivals, it should remain in the fourth position on Rosh Hashanah. The methods of both R. Akiba and R. Yoḥanan accomplish this. Korban Ha'edah suggests that the logic behind this position is to juxtapose Sanctification (of the Name) to Sanctification (of the Day).

68. To seal the third benediction, "the Sanctification of the Name," on Rosh Hashanah.

69. To seal the third benediction. The additional phrase is included to stress the "pardoning" aspect of the day.

70. These two phrases seal the fourteenth benediction. Hence in the Palestinian ritual the fourteenth benediction, "Build the House," and the fifteenth, the "Blessing of David," were combined. See Palestinian Talmud Berakhot, chapter 4, Halakhah 3.

71. In the benediction which follows the reading of the prophetic portion this seal is to be used.

72. The reference is to the benediction known as "Sanctification of the Day." In the paragraph which begins Vatitten lanu (and You have given us . . .), the holiness of that particular festival is proclaimed. One position holds that the paragraph should read: "And You have given us in love, O Lord our God . . . this Day of Memorial . . . and this Sabbath Day . . . Blessed art Thou, O Lord, Who sanctifies the Sabbath."

73. Seal with "Blessed art Thou, O Lord, Who sanctifies Israel and the Day of Memorial."

74. "And You have given us in love, O Lord our God . . . this Sabbath Day . . . and this Day of Memorial . . . Blessed art Thou, O Lord, Who sanctifies the Sabbath."

Halakhah 7

1. They may not recite fewer than ten Sovereignty Verses—corresponding to the ten expressions of praise that David uttered: *Hallelujah. Praise God in His sanctuary; Praise Him in the firmament of His power*, etc., until *Let every thing that has breath praise the Lord. Hallelujah.*[75]

2. [They may not recite fewer] than ten Remembrance Verses—corresponding to the ten expressions of confession that Isaiah uttered: *Wash you, make you clean, put away [the evil of your doings from before My eyes]*, etc.; *Learn to do well; seek justice*, etc.; what is written after it? *Come now, and let us reason together, saith the Lord*, etc.[76]

3. [They may not recite fewer] than ten Shofar Verses—corresponding to the seven lambs, the bullock, the ram, and the goat.[77]

4. Biblical verses containing the word *El, Elohim*, etc. are accounted to him for the purpose of Sovereignty Verses; the words of Rabbi Jose. Rabbi Judah says: they are not accounted to him.[78]

Biblical verses containing the word *El, Elohim*, etc. as well as mention of Sovereignty are accounted to him for the purpose of two [verses]; the words of Rabbi Jose. Rabbi Judah says: they are not accounted to him.[79]

Sing praises to God, sing praises; sing praises to our King, sing praises—accounted to him for the purpose of two [verses]; the words of Rabbi Jose. Rabbi Judah says: they are not accounted to him.[79]

5. Rabbi Zeira asked: is it with regard to it and that which

75. In Psalms 150, the order to praise God is found ten times in addition to the opening and closing "Hallelujah." Verse 3 reads: *Praise Him with the sound of the shofar.*

76. Is. 1:16–18. Korban Ha'edah points out that these are not "expressions of confession" strictly speaking, but rather represent ten modes of repentance. Verse 18, *Come now, and let us reason together*, is appropriate for Rosh Hashanah because it is a day of judgment and confession, of reconciliation with God.

77. The offerings to be made on Rosh Hashanah.

78. The text has R. Judah making the affirmative statement and R. Jose making the negative. However Rabinovitz, *Sha'are* . . . , p. 280 suggests switching the textual order in the first and third statement here because in the Tosefta parallel and the Babli it is R. Jose who always takes the more lenient position, with R. Judah being the nay-sayer. I have followed his suggestion.

79. Except as one verse.

follows it that they differ, or is it with regard to it itself that they differ?[80]

[We learn the answer] from that which is taught in a *baraita*: everyone acknowledges with regard to the verse *God reigns over the nations, [God sits upon the throne of His holiness]* (Psalm 47:9) that this is [accounted as] one. So this proves that it is with regard to it and that which follows it that they differ.[81]

6.   *Lift up your heads, O ye gates,*
       And be ye lifted up, ye everlasting doors;
       [That the King of glory may come in.
       "Who is the King of glory?"
       "The Lord strong and mighty,
       The Lord mighty in battle."] (Psalms 24:7–8)

       Lift up your heads, O ye gates,
       Yea, lift them up, ye everlasting doors;
       [That the King of glory may come in.
       "Who is the King of glory?"
       "The Lord of hosts;
       He is the King of glory." Selah] (Psalms 24:9–10)

The first[82] is for the purpose of one, and the second[83] for the purpose of two; the words of Rabbi Judah. Rabbi Jose says: the first[82] is for the purpose of two, and the second[83] for the purpose of three.[84]

7. Rabbi Yoḥanan ben Nuri said: if one recited three, he has fulfilled his obligation. We used to think to say: three from each one [of the three categories]. But it was found to be taught [in a *baraita*]:[85] even three from all of them [together], he has fulfilled his obligation.

---

80. Psalms 47:7 has within it the words "God" and "King." Verse 8 reads: *Because God is King of all the earth, sing praises with understanding.* Hence the question is whether Jose and Judah are trying to determine whether to account verse 7 as one or two Sovereignty Verses because the words "God" and "King" appear there, or whether to account verses 7 and 8 together as one or two Sovereignty Verses, since, as Korban Ha'edah points out, they go together like the "a" and "b" part of a verse.

81. Since everyone acknowledges that Psalms 47:9, which contains the word "God" twice, is nonetheless considered as one Sovereignty Verse, verse 47:7, which contains the words "God" and "King," should likewise be considered as one. Therefore, the question must be whether to consider verses 7 and 8 together as one or two Sovereignty Verses.

82. Psalms 24:7–8.

83. Psalms 24:9–10.

84. According to Korban Ha'edah, R. Judah does not count the phrase "Who is the King of glory?" either time, whereas R. Jose does.

85. Tosefta Rosh Hashanah 2:12.

8. They may not mention Remembrance, Sovereignty, or Shofar Verses which deal with divine retribution. Remembrance, as it is written, *Did not the Lord remember them?* etc. (Jeremiah 44:21).[86] Sovereignty, as it is written, *As I live, says the Lord God, surely with a mighty hand, [and with an outstretched arm, and with fury poured out, will I rule over you]* (Ezekial 20:33–34). Shofar, as it is written, *Because you have heard, O my soul, the sound of the shofar, the alarm of war* (Jeremiah 4:19).

9. One begins with [verses from] the Pentateuch, and concludes with [verses from] the Prophets. [Rabbi Jose says: if one concludes with verses from the Pentateuch, he has fulfilled his obligation.][87] What? Ex post facto? But ab initio no? Said Rabbi Yoḥanan, so is the Mishnah to be read: Rabbi Jose says, it is necessary to conclude with [verses from] the Pentateuch.

Halakhah 8[88]

1. Rabbi Jacob bar Aḥa [said] in the name of Rabbi Yoḥanan: because of an event that took place.[89] Once they sounded the shofar during the initial [morning prayers], but their enemies assumed that they were marching against them, so they arose against them and killed them.

Because they see them reading the *Shema*, praying [the *Amidah*], reading the Pentateuch, praying [the Additional Service], and sounding the shofar, they say: they are engaged in their religious observances.[90]

2. And say that the same is the case with the Hallel![91] All the people are not there.[92]

86. What the Lord "remembered" in this context were the offerings of incense and drink that the people made to the Queen of Heaven in the cities of Judah and the streets of Jerusalem. Because of their abominations, God punished them.

87. Mishnah R.H. 4:8.

88. On Mishnah 9 in the Leiden MS, Mishnah 7 in the printed Mishnah texts.

89. They established the Shofar Service as part of the Additional Service rather than as part of the Morning Service.

90. And hence the second one, the reader of the Additional Service, sounds the shofar.

91. The Mishnah continues: "but at times when the *Hallel* is recited, the first one recites the *Hallel*." The question being raised is why the same logic which is applied to the shofar doesn't hold for the *Hallel* also. Would not their enemies, seeing and hearing such a tumult in the synagogue so early in the morning, assume this to be an incendiary gathering?

92. P'ne Moshe understands the response to mean that on those days when the *Hallel* is read, the crowds are not as great as those of the New Year, and

3. And say that even with regard to the sounding of the shofar likewise all the people are not there![93]

Said Rabbi Jonah: it is written, *yet they seek me daily* (Isaiah 58:2)—this refers to the sounding of the shofar and the willow-branch.[94]

4. Rabbi Joshua ben Levi in the name of Rabbi Alexandri learned it[95] from this: *Hear the right, O Lord* (Psalms 17:1)—that refers to the *Shema*.[96] *Attend unto my cry*—that refers to the chanting of [the section from] the Pentateuch. *Give ear unto my prayer*—that refers to the *Amidah*. *From lips without deceit*—that refers to the Additional Service. What is written after it? *Let my judgment come forth from Thy presence.*[97]

5. Said Rabbi Aḥa bar Pappa before Rabbi Zeira: it is different,[98] for the religious act of the day is in the Additional Service. Said Rabbi Taḥlifa of Caesarea: a scriptural verse established this: *it is a day of sounding the shofar . . . and you shall make [a burnt offering]* (Numbers 29:1–2).[99]

6. Rabbi Eleazar the son of Rabbi Jose in the name of Rabbi Jose the son of a laundress: with regard to all of the other offerings it is written: *and you shall offer [a burnt offering]*, but here it is written *and you shall make [a burnt offering]*; God said to them, since you entered into judgment before me on the Holiday of the New Year, and you departed in peace,[100] I attribute it to you as if you were made as a new creature.[101]

---

hence the surrounded enemies would not feel so threatened. Korban Ha'edah understands the response differently: "Are not all the people there?!" He surmises that perhaps, because of the maxim *in the multitude of people is the King's glory* (Prov. 14:28), the *Hallel* should be moved to the Additional Service because more people would be present later. But the answer is that everyone is already there for the Morning Service.

93. If in fact not everyone comes even on Rosh Hashanah, those surrounding enemies who might have presumed a war gathering if they saw total attendance and then heard the shofar sounded would have no basis for anxiety.

94. The proof-text tells us that the people *are* all there on Rosh Hashanah, unlike those days when the *Hallel* is read.

95. That the shofar should be sounded during the Additional Service.

96. According to P'ne Moshe, it is "right" for them to rise early in order to recite the *Shema* at its proper time.

97. This is understood as the sounding of the shofar since the shofar serves to remind God of Israel's merit at the time of judgment.

98. The sounding of the shofar is different from the reading of the *Hallel*, in that still another reason exists for placing it in the Additional Service.

99. The sounding of the shofar is juxtaposed to the Additional Offering to teach that it is to be sounded at *Musaf* time.

100. That is, the good deeds overbalanced the sins.

101. For the Additional Offering on Rosh Hashanah, Scripture uses a different verb, "you shall make," to set it off from the other offerings. And in a post-Temple period, this distinction becomes even more significant, since the best

Rabbi M'sharsh'ya in the name of Rabbi Idi: with regard to all of the [other] offerings it is written "sin,"[102] but with regard to the Feast of Weeks it is not written "sin"; God said to them, since you accepted upon yourselves the yoke of the Law, I attribute it to you as if you had not sinned all of your days.

Halakhah 9

1. So is the Mishnah to be read: not with an implement the use of which is prohibited because of the law of Sabbath rest and not with an implement the use of which is prohibited because of an explicit biblical prohibition.[103]

2. Said Rabbi Eleazar: our Mishnah[104] is dealing with an adult on the Holiday of the New Year which happened to fall on the Sabbath. And it is taught as follows: they practice [even] on the Sabbath in order to learn to sound the shofar; "they should not prevent children from sounding the shofar" on the festival day.[105]

---

offering that one can make on the Day of Judgment is one's own contrite spirit. One who offers his own soul with sincerity is as if created anew.

102. In Numbers, chapters 28 and 29, the offerings for the Sabbath, the New Moon, Passover, the Feast of Weeks, the New Year Festival, the Day of Atonement, and the Festival of Booths are spelled out. The offerings for each of these days except for the Festival of Weeks include a he-goat for a sin-offering (see Num. 28:15, 22; 29:5, 11, 16, 22, 28, 34). The he-goat to be offered for the Feast of Weeks is not termed a "sin-offering," although it is "to make atonement for you" (see Num. 28:30). The assumption of the text is that the term "sin" is not applied to the offering for the Feast of Weeks because that is the day of the receiving of Torah on Sinai, and this act served to override all of Israel's sins.

103. I have translated according to the interpretation suggested in P'ne Moshe and in Rabinovitz, Sha'are . . . , p. 280. Babli R.H. 33a explains why both categories are mentioned. An instrument prohibited for shaping a shofar because of the law of Sabbath rest might be a sickle, which is not normally used for this purpose and hence would not be forbidden as "work" in the legal sense. An instrument prohibited because of pentateuchal sanction might be a knife, which would normally be used for cutting. The Mishnah mentions both categories as if to say "the rabbinically prohibited and how much the more so the scripturally prohibited."

104. The subject under discussion is "they should not prevent children. . . ."

105. A *baraita* is introduced to strengthen the opinion of R. Eleazar. It understands the second phrase, "rather they should practice with them until they learn," to mean that an adult teaching a child to sound the shofar may continue the lessons even on the Sabbath. The first phrase, "they should not prevent children from sounding the shofar," refers to those children who are blowing on Rosh Hashanah, but not with a teacher and not for educational purposes.

Halakhah 10

1. If he did them in one breath?[106] It is found that it was taught in a *baraita*: if he did them in one breath, he has fulfilled his obligation.

But are we not taught in our Mishnah: the manner of shofar soundings is three series of three blasts each?[107] [This means] that there should not be less.[108]

2. Rabbi Zeira [in the name of] Rabbi Abba bar Ilai in the name of Rav: it is necessary to sound a quivering note immediately after a sustained note.[109] Rabbi Abba in the name of Abba bar Rav Huna: it is not necessary to sound a quivering note *immediately* after a sustained note.

3. What is the definition of a quivering note? Rabbi Ḥananiah and Rabbi Mana [disagreed]: one said, like the trimeter;[110] and the other said, three short notes. Rabbi Ḥananiah was suspicious of that definition of Rabbi Mana as well as his own.[111]

4. And what [Mishnah] says this?[112] "If first one sounds a sustained blast, and then sustains the second to the equivalent of two, it is accounted to him as one blast only."[113] Rabbi Abba bar Z'mina in the name of Rabbi Zeira: even one blast is not reck-

(59d)

106. A series of three blasts which consists of a sustained, a quivering, and a sustained note. The question, phrased differently, is whether one can go through all three of the separate sounds without pausing to breathe and fulfill one's obligation, or whether a distinct pause between each of the blows is required.

107. And if he did a series in one breath he would not be sounding three separate blasts in a series.

108. In total duration of time that the blasts are sustained. But the Mishnah says nothing about incumbent pauses within the series.

109. That is, without a pause, in one breath.

110. According to Jastrow, p. 553, a trimeter is "a verse of three iambic meters." Hence here, when the texts says "*like* the trimeter," it means short-long, short-long, etc.

111. I have followed the emendation suggested by Rabinovitz, *Shaʾare* . . . , p. 280. According to Korban Haʾedah, because R. Ḥananiah was uncomfortable with his own definition and that of R. Mana, he sounded three series of short blasts and then three series of long blasts.

112. What is the basis for the position that one has not fulfilled his obligation until he has heard the entire blast from beginning to end? This paragraph from chapter 4, Halakhah 10, repeats the last paragraph from chapter 3, Halakhah 3. The comment in chapter 3 is on the end of Mishnah 3 : 2, where it says that the shofar is sounded for a long note, and the trumpets are sounded for a short note. Korban Haʾedah points out that the full blast must be heard to fulfill one's responsibility. Hence we must understand the Mishnah to mean that first the trumpets are sounded for a short note, and when they are completely finished the shofar is sounded for a long note.

113. Mishnah R.H. 4 : 11.

oned to him. Why? The beginning is joined to the end, and the end is joined to the beginning. The beginning has no end, and the end has no beginning.[114]

5. If they are sounding the shofar in one place,[115] and reciting the benedictions in another,[116] some authorities teach: he should betake himself to the one who is sounding the shofar. Other authorities teach: [he should betake himself] to the one who is reciting the benedictions. Regarding the one who says that he should betake himself to the one who is sounding the shofar, this applies if there would not otherwise be enough time for the sounding of the shofar.[117] Regarding the one who says that he should betake himself to the one who is reciting the benedictions, this applies if there would be enough time in the day for the sounding of the shofar.[118]

6. We learn it[119] from that which Rabbi Jacob bar Idi said in the name of Rabbi Joshua ben Levi: if they are sounding the shofar in one place, and reciting the benedictions in another, he should betake himself to the one who is sounding the shofar, and he should not betake himself to the one who is reciting the benedictions.[120]

7. And what authority teaches this?[121] When the Holiday of the New Year happened to fall on a Sabbath, and they were

114. Each individual *tekiah* requires its own distinct beginning and end. In this instance, the final *tekiah* of one set is combined with the first *tekiah* of the next set. But the *tekiah* which constitutes the first half of the blast does not have its own end, the second half, its own beginning. Hence "even one blast is not reckoned to him," since it is not a valid blast. The one blast mentioned in Mishnah R.H. 4:11 refers rather to the first *tekiah* in the set.

115. According to the explanation of Korban Ha'edah, they do not say the benedictions here because they do not know how to recite them properly.

116. But they do not sound the shofar here.

117. Time would not suffice to go first to the place where they are reciting the benedictions and then to the place where they are sounding the shofar. Since the obligation to hear the shofar is scriptural, whereas the obligation regarding the benedictions is rabbinic, he proceeds to hear the shofar.

118. And hence the two positions do not contradict each other. In this instance, he goes first to the place where they are reciting the benedictions lest the time for public worship pass. Afterwards he goes to the place where they are sounding the shofar.

119. The first tannaitic position stated above.

120. P'ne Moshe points out that the mention of R. Joshua ben Levi's position here would be superfluous in the light of the first tannaitic position above unless he were saying something different—that one may always go to the one who is sounding the shofar, irrespective of the time of day. The doing of the toraitic *mitzvah* exempts him from the additional burden of pursuing the rabbinic benedictions. Hence the contradiction stands.

121. The second tannaitic position stated above.

sounding the shofar in one place, and reciting the benedictions in another, he should betake himself to the one who is reciting the benedictions, and he should not betake himself to the one who is sounding the *shofar*.[122] Why? Because everyone knows how to sound the shofar,[123] but not everyone knows how to recite the benedictions.

Another interpretation:[124] an individual can act effectively on behalf of his fellow with regard to the sounding of the shofar, but an individual cannot act effectively on behalf of his fellow with regard to the benedictions.[125]

8. "When the Holiday of the New Year happened to fall on a Sabbath . . ."—is this not like the one for whom there would not otherwise be enough time for the sounding of the shofar, and yet you say he should betake himself to the one who is reciting the benedictions? This proves that the Tannaim did in fact disagree.[126]

122. According to Korban Ha'edah, the point of the *baraita* is that prior to the onset of this New Year's Day that happened to fall on a Sabbath, the individual had to select between one of the two locations to which he would betake himself. He could not go to the two places, since our Mishnah teaches that "for the sake of the shofar of the New Year, one does not transgress the Sabbath limit." So he must choose between the one who is reciting the benedictions and the one who is sounding the shofar.

123. Surely he would be able to find someone there who could blow the shofar for him.

124. Of the second tannaitic position that he should betake himself to the one who is reciting the benedictions.

125. An individual may sound the shofar for another, and the hearer fulfills his obligation for shofar. The reader of the congregation in the context of ten worshippers absolves the public of their obligation for the benedictions. Hence he must find a congregation before the time for worship has passed.

126. In the translation and explanation which appears in the text from paragraphs 5 through 8 above, I have carefully followed the manuscript as it exists. Rabinovitz, Sha'are . . . , pp. 280–81, has done some textual emendation and rearrangement of the order of the material to arrive at a smoother reading and more cogent text. I will include here his reworking in its entirety:

They are sounding the shofar in one place, and reciting the benedictions in another. Some authorities teach: he should betake himself to the one who is sounding the shofar. Other authorities teach: regarding the one who is reciting the benedictions. What is the case? Regarding the one who says that he should betake himself to the one who is sounding the shofar, this applies if there would not otherwise be enough time for the sounding of the shofar. Regarding the one who says that he should betake himself to the one who is reciting the benedictions, this applies if there would be enough time in the day for the sounding of the shofar.

We learn it from that which R. Jacob bar Idi said in the name of R. Joshua ben Levi: if they are sounding the shofar in one place, and reciting the benedictions in another, he should betake himself to the one who is reciting the benedictions, and he should not betake himself to the one who is sounding the shofar.

9. Rabban Gamaliel says: the reader of the congregation absolves the public of their obligation.[127] Rabbi Huna senior of Sephoris said in the name of Rabbi Yohanan: the Law is according to Rabban Gamaliel with regard to those prayers on the New Year interspersed with blowing of the shofar.[128]

10. Rabbi Zeira and Rav Ḥisda were sitting there[129] during the prayers interspersed with the blowing of the shofar. When they had finished their prayers, Rav Ḥisda arose wanting to pray. Rabbi Zeira said to him: did we not already pray? He said to him: I pray and then pray again. For some individuals had come down from the West,[130] and they said in the name of Rabbi Yohanan: the Law is according to Rabban Gamaliel with regard to those prayers on the New Year interspersed with blowing the shofar. But I did not have proper devotional attention.[131] If I had achieved proper devotional attention, I would have fulfilled my religious obligation.[132]

Said Rabbi Zeira: and it is right.[133] For whereas all of the Tannaim teach it in the name of Rabban Gamaliel, Rabbi Hoshaya teaches it in the name of the Sages.[134]

Why? Because everyone knows how to sound the shofar, but not everyone knows how to recite the benedictions.

Another interpretation: an individual can act effectively on behalf of his fellow with regard to the sounding of the shofar, but an individual cannot act effectively on behalf of his fellow with regard to the benedictions.

You can meet this difficulty by saying that it is like the one who said he should betake himself to the one who is reciting the benedictions.

And what authority teaches this? When the Holiday of the New Year happened to fall on a Sabbath, and they were sounding the shofar in one place, and reciting the benedictions in another, he should betake himself to the one who is reciting the benedictions, and he should not betake himself to the one who is sounding the shofar.

"When the Holiday of the New Year happened to fall on a Sabbath . . ."—is this not like the one for whom there would not otherwise be enough time for the sounding of the shofar, and yet you say he should betake himself to the one who is reciting the benedictions? This proves that the Tannaim did in fact disagree.

127. That is, the one who officiates aloud at the service exempts the other worshipers from repeating the prayers.

128. Those prayers which are said before the shofar is sounded during the *musaf* service, i.e. the Sovereignty, Remembrance, and Shofar sections of the *musaf*.

129. In Babylonia.

130. That is, had come to Babylonia from Palestine.

131. During the recitation of the prayers by the reader of the congregation.

132. By following the prayers of the reader of the congregation, and I would not have begun to pray a second time.

133. That these various sages taught that the Law is according to the position articulated by Rabban Gamaliel.

134. Which establishes it as Law.

11. Rabbi Ada of Caesarea said in the name of Rabbi Yoḥanan: assuming that he was there from the beginning of the service.[135]

Said Rabbi Tanḥum in the name of Rabbi Jeremiah: Our Mishnah itself teaches this. "The order of the Benedictions [for the Rosh Hashanah *Musaf*]: one says "the Patriarchs," "the Powers," and "the Sanctification of God's name."[136]

135. The reader of the congregation absolves him of his obligation.

136. Therefore one must be present already for these first three of the eighteen benedictions, if the recitation by the reader of the congregation is to suffice to absolve him of his obligation.

Index of Biblical and Talmudic References

Bible

2 Chronicles
3:2, 13–15

Daniel
8:12, 93
9:21, 36
10:1, 15
10:6, 66
10:12, 91
10:21, 36

Deuteronomy
2:5, 21
4:7–8, 43
11:12, 47
12:5–6, 22–23
15:1, 36
15:19, 35
15:20, 25
23:22, 25, 29
23:24, 24, 30
32:20, 94

Esther
2:16, 36

Exodus
6:13, 90
12:1, 4, 49
12:2, 2, 13–14,
    31–32, 75, 79
17:11, 8, 77

19:1, 15
20:33–34, 110
23:16, 35
23:18, 25
24:9, 57
34:22, 35
40:17, 18, 31

Ezekiel
13:9, 71
40:1, 15

Genesis
1:5, 74
1:8, 13
1:14, 74
6:14, 94
8:13, 17
21:17, 42
24:21, 52

Habbakuk
3:10, 93
3:11, 93

Haggai
1:1, 15
1:15, 16
2:15, 16

Hosea
8:3, 94

Isaiah
5:2, 65
6:2, 36
6:6, 36
47:4, 54
58:2, 111

Jeremiah
4:19, 110
34:14, 90
44:21, 110

Job
7:18, 40
8:6, 43
11:11, 42
24:9, 47
25:2, 66
38:26, 47

Joshua
5:2, 94
6:5, 77, 85

1 Kings
2:11, 19
6:1, 15
6:37, 36
6:38, 36
8:2, 36
8:59, 40
9:10, 15
11:16, 21

2 Kings
15:13, 19

Leviticus
12:3, 29
17:4, 29
19:23, 3
19:24, 37
19:32, 43
22:9, 43
23:1–2, 1
23:2, 44, 79, 82
23:4, 7, 12, 44,
    52, 57, 82
23:8, 103
23:22, 87
23:23–25, 1
23:24, 35, 87–
    88, 99
23:38, 21–22
23:40, 102–3
25:8, 36
25:9, 36, 87–88,
    100
25:10, 68, 89
27:33, 27

Nehemiah
1:1, 18, 36
2:1, 18, 36

Numbers
6:10, 27

9:1, 15
10:2, 94
10:5, 89
10:6, 89
10:7, 89
10:10, 1
10:11, 18
21:8, 8, 77–
    78, 94
21:9, 94
28:14, 31–32
29:1, 88, 99–100
29:1–2, 100, 111
29:1–6, 2
29:19, 116
29:31, 46
29:33, 46
29:39, 22
33:3, 74
33:38, 15

Proverbs
4:2, 94
21:3, 20
23:23, 94
30:31, 43
31:14, 90

Psalms
5:6, 42
9:9, 40

12:7, 48
17:1, 111
24:7–8, 109
24:9–10, 109
33:15, 11, 46
65:11, 47
65:14, 32
69:32, 85
81:2, 104
81:2–5, 2
81:4, 2
81:5, 2, 44
81:7, 104
103:9, 43
104:19, 74
144:14, 74

1 Samuel
3:14, 70
12:6, 73

2 Samuel
5:5, 19
7:12, 20

Zechariah
1:1, 16

Mishnah
Rosh Hashanah
1:1, 2, 11

1:1–2, 2
1:1–3, 2–3
1:2, 11
1:3, 3, 11
1:4, 3, 11
1:4–3:1, 3–8
1:5, 4, 11
1:6, 4, 12
1:7, 4, 12
1:8, 12
1:8–9, 4
1:9, 4, 12
1:10, 4, 12
1:11, 5, 12
2:1, 5, 55
2:2, 5, 55–56
2:3, 5, 56
2:4, 56
2:4–5, 5
2:5, 56
2:6, 56
2:6–7, 6
2:7, 56–57
2:8, 6, 57
2:9, 6, 57
2:10, 57
2:10–11, 7
2:11, 57
2–12, 7, 57–58
3:1, 7–8, 76
3:2, 8, 76–77

3:2–4:11, 8–10
3:3, 8, 77
3:4, 8, 77
3:5, 8, 77
3:6, 8, 77
3:7, 77
3:7–8, 8
3:8, 77–78
3:9, 9, 79
4:1, 9, 96
4:2, 9, 96–97
4:3, 9, 97
4:4, 9, 97
4:5, 9, 97–98
4:6, 98
4:6–7, 9
4:7, 98
4:8, 9, 98
4:9, 9, 98
4:10, 10, 98–99
4:11, 10, 99

Sanhedrin
3:3, 51

Terumot
10:8, 52

General Index

Abba: four new years, 24; shofar, sounding of, 107; witnesses to new moon, 67, 78–79, 84
Abba bar Abba, witnesses to new moon, 92
Abba b. R. Huna, shofar, sounding of, 107, 113
Abba bar Ilai, shofar, sounding of, 113
Abba bar Jeremiah, shofar, sounding of, 107
Abba bar Mammal, four new years, 27, 37
Abba Mari, four new years, 26
Abba bar Pappa, shofar, sounding of, 99
Abba bar Z'bida, witnesses to new moon, 69, 71
Abba bar Z'mina: shofar, sounding of, 113; witnesses to new moon, 86, 92
Abbahu: four new years, 25, 33; shofar, sounding of, 106; witnesses to new moon, 50, 63, 84
Abbayi, witnesses to new moon, 53
Abbina, witnesses to new moon, 93
Abun: four new years, 24, 46; witnesses to new moon, 54, 66
Abun bar Ḥiyya, four new years, 24, 27, 34
Ada, shofar, sounding of, 117
Ada of Caesarea, shofar, sounding of, 104
Aḥa: four new years, 14, 25; witnesses to new moon, 53, 94–95
Aḥa bar Pappa, shofar, sounding of, 104, 111

Akiba: four new years, 12, 32, 38, 46; shofar, sounding of, 98, 105–6; witnesses to new moon, 48–49, 57, 72–73, 81, 88
Alexandri, shofar, sounding of, 111
Ami: four new years, 27; witnesses to new moon, 60, 69, 78, 82

Bar Kapara, witnesses to new moon, 66
Ben Azzai, four new years, 32–35
Berakia: four new years, 46; witnesses to new moon, 74, 84

David, reign as king, 19–21
Dosa ben Harkinas, witnesses to new moon, 57

Eleazar: four new years, 11, 16–18, 21, 27, 32, 35–39, 43, 46; shofar, sounding of, 96, 106, 111–12; witnesses to new moon, 51–52, 65, 71
Eleazar b. R. Zadok, witnesses to new moon, 57, 71
Eudemus Neḥota, four new years, 28

Festival of New Year, 21–35
Four New Years, 2–3, 11–47

Gamaliel: four new years, 12, 38–39; shofar, sounding of, 99, 116; witnesses to new moon, 49, 57–58, 72, 74
Gamaliel the Elder, witnesses to new moon, 56, 65

Haggai: four new years, 29; witnesses
    to new moon, 69
Hama, four new years, 30, 44
Hama bar Hanina, witnesses to new
    moon, 94
Hananiah: four new years, 42; shofar,
    sounding of, 113
Hananiah b. R. Hillel, four new
    years, 28
Hananiah b. Jose the Galilean, shofar,
    sounding of, 106
Hanin bar Abba, shofar, sounding of,
    107
Hanina: four new years, 14, 16, 25,
    36; witnesses to new moon, 67, 69
Hanina b. Jose the Galilean, witnesses
    to new moon, 81
Helbo, witnesses to new moon, 71
Hillel, House of, four new years, 11,
    34, 37–38
Hisda: shofar, sounding of, 116; wit-
    nesses to new moon, 48, 81
Hiyya, witnesses to new moon, 78, 92
Hiyya bar Abba: four new years, 41,
    43, 45; shofar, sounding of, 105;
    witnesses to new moon, 67, 69–
    70, 72
Hiyya bar Ada, witnesses to new
    moon, 53, 68
Hiyya the Great, witnesses to new
    moon, 67
Hiyya bar Jose, four new years, 14
Hiyya bar Madya, witnesses to new
    moon, 69
Hoshaya: four new years, 38, 44;
    shofar, sounding of, 116
Huna: four new years, 20, 32, 35;
    shofar, sounding of, 116; witnesses
    to new moon, 51–52, 59, 64,
    83–84

Idi, shofar, sounding of, 112
Ila: four new years, 22, 26, 38, 44;
    shofar, sounding of, 104; witnesses
    to new moon, 90
Isaac, four new years, 17, 40, 45
Isaac bar Ketsatstah, four new
    years, 20
Isaac bar Nahman: four new years, 14;
    witnesses to new moon, 87
Ishmael, four new years, 26, 33

Ishmael b. Yohanan ben Beroqah;
    shofar, sounding of, 105; witnesses
    to new moon, 81, 89
Issachar, four new years, 42

Jacob bar Aha: four new years, 13–14;
    shofar, sounding of, 107, 110; wit-
    nesses to new moon, 69–70, 82, 92
Jacob bar Idi, shofar, sounding of, 114
Jacob bar Susi, witnesses to new
    moon, 54
Jeremiah: four new years, 33; shofar,
    sounding of, 117
Jonah: four new years, 14, 16, 18–20,
    25, 29, 31, 33, 35–36; shofar,
    sounding of, 100–101, 103, 111;
    witnesses to new moon, 52, 58, 64,
    67, 69, 85–87
Jose: four new years, 12–14, 26–29,
    34, 36–38, 40; shofar, sounding
    of, 98, 102, 108–9, 111; wit-
    nesses to new moon, 49, 51–52,
    54, 58, 64, 69, 72, 76, 82, 85–87,
    89–90, 94
Jose b. Abun: four new years, 27, 32,
    39; witnesses to new moon, 61
Jose ben Hanina, witnesses to new
    moon, 92
Jose b. R. N'horai, witnesses to new
    moon, 95
Joshua, witnesses to new moon, 57, 72
Joshua ben Korhah, shofar, sounding
    of, 97
Joshua b. Levi: four new years, 42;
    shofar, sounding of, 102, 104, 107,
    111, 114; witnesses to new moon,
    48, 78, 86–87, 93
Josiah, four new years, 31
Judah: shofar, sounding of, 108–9;
    witnesses to new moon, 49, 59, 77,
    84, 90–91
Judah the Cappadocian, witnesses to
    new moon, 54
Judah Gozrayah, witnesses to new
    moon, 94
Judah the Patriarch: shofar, sounding
    of, 107; witnesses to new moon, 80
Judah bar Pazzi: shofar, sounding of,
    107; witnesses to new moon, 82–
    83, 94
Judah bar Shalom, four new years, 21

Kahana: four new years, 31, 47; shofar, sounding of, 99; witnesses to new moon, 69–70
K'rispa, four new years, 41, 44

Levi: four new years, 28, 40, 44, 46; shofar, sounding of, 99–100; witnesses to new moon, 66, 94

Mana: four new years, 14, 34–35, 38; shofar, sounding of, 113; witnesses to new moon, 51
Mattaniah, witnesses to new moon, 60
Meir: four new years, 32; witnesses to new moon, 52, 54, 94
Mesha, four new years, 33
Messengers dispatched because of six new moons, 47–95
M'sharsh'ya, shofar, sounding of, 112

Nathan, witnesses to new moon, 91–92
Nehemiah, witnesses to new moon, 50
N'horai, witnesses to new moon, 61
Nisan as start of new year, 13–18

Rav: four new years, 40; shofar, sounding of, 107, 113; witnesses to new moon, 59, 71, 80
Reign of Kings, 19–21

Samuel, four new years, 15
Samuel bar Isaac: four new years, 31, 33, 36; witnesses to new moon, 83, 90
Samuel b. R. Jose, four new years, 30
Samuel b. R. Jose b. Judah, four new years, 23
Samuel bar Nahman: four new years, 20; shofar, sounding of, 104; witnesses to new moon, 82
Shammai, House of, four new years, 11, 34, 37–38

Shila, witnesses to new moon, 74
Shofar, sounding of, 8–10, 96–117
Simon: four new years, 11, 21–22, 32, 34, 42, 44; shofar, sounding of, 102; witnesses to new moon, 49, 74
Simon b. Gamaliel: shofar, sounding of, 106; witnesses to new moon, 81
Simon bar Karsana, four new years, 14
Simon ben Lakish: shofar, sounding of, 99; witnesses to new moon, 52–53, 69–71, 74–75
Simon b. Yohai: four new years, 46; shofar, sounding of, 100; witnesses to new moon, 66, 68

Tabi, four new years, 31
Tahlifa, shofar, sounding of, 111
Tanhum, shofar, sounding of, 117
Tishri as New Year for Years, 35–39

Witnesses to new moon, 3–8, 47–95
World judged four times yearly, 39–47

Yohanan: four new years, 13–14, 37, 41, 44; shofar, sounding of, 99, 104–5, 110, 116–17; witnesses to new moon, 57, 65–66, 69–70, 74–75, 82, 87, 90–92
Yohanan ben Nuri: shofar, sounding of, 98, 105–6, 109; witnesses to new moon, 81
Yohanan ben Zakkai, shofar, sounding of, 96–98, 102–3

Z'bida, witnesses to new moon, 69
Zechariah, four new years, 28
Zeira: four new years, 24, 27, 37–38; shofar, sounding of, 99, 104, 107–8, 111, 113, 116; witnesses to new moon, 59, 63–64, 78–81, 83, 86–87, 91–92

DATE DUE

OCT 1 2 2006			
OCT 1 7 2011			
GAYLORD			PRINTED IN U.S.A.